EUROPEAN HOUSE NOW

D1517717

EUROPEAN HOUSE NOW

CONTEMPORARY ARCHITECTURAL DIRECTIONS

SUSAN DOUBILET AND DARALICE BOLES

UNIVERSE

First published in the United States of America in 1999 by UNIVERSE PUBLISHING

A Division of Rizzoli International Publications, Inc.

300 Park Avenue South New York, NY 10010

99 00 01 02 / 10 9 8 7 6 5 4 3 2 1

Library of Congress Cataloging–in–Publication Data

   European house now : contemporary architectural directions / Susan Doubilet and Daralice Boles.

      p.   cm.

   ISBN 0-7893-0359-0

   1. Architecture, Domestic—Europe. 2. Architecture, Modern—20th century—Europe. I. Boles,
Daralice D. (Daralice Donkervoet) II. Title.

   NA7325.D86 1999

  728'.094'09049—dc21   99-34203 CIP

Photograph on page 5: House in Vaise, France, Jourda Perraudin, Architects, photograph © Archipress, Paris

Design: Group C Inc New Haven/Boston (BC, FS, EZ)

Printed in Italy

CONTENTS

INTRODUCTION

SUSAN DOUBILET   DARALICE BOLES

The twenty-nine houses featured in this book were designed by twenty-six European architecture firms and were built during the last fifteen years of the twentieth century. As in this book's predecessor, *American House Now* (Universe, 1997), these houses were chosen because they represent design excellence in and of themselves, and because they exemplify the richness and variety of the modern movement at the end of the twentieth century.

The subject of house design is a delightful one, and one that interests almost everyone, from the average person who can imagine living in one or another of the houses on these pages, to architects who are inspired by exceptional house designs. It should be noted, however, that the inspiration provided by designs such as these is not merely visual. The very nature of the problem of designing a single-family house focuses on the central issue of all architecture: namely, the definition of a human place within this universe. Furthermore, the individual house is unparalleled as a laboratory for design ideas. It allows architects to experiment on a small scale with new materials and technologies and permits them to develop pragmatic prototypes, such as prefabricated building parts or ecologically sensitive designs, that can be extended to larger scale problems. Because the client for a house is almost always a highly motivated individual or couple closely identifying with the chosen architect's design philosophy, private houses are often executed with little compromise to that philosophy. For this reason, the study of houses offers a representative reading of architectural thought at a given time.

EUROPEAN...

It should come as no surprise that the European-designed houses featured in this book all represent a modern approach. This approach is one that expresses structure, materials, or function in a direct fashion, and that seeks to set itself apart from the architecture of any previous era. With a few notable exceptions, European architects have remained faithful to the modern movement in one form or another ever since that style's emergence as a dominant force in the early twentieth century, so much so that modernism has effectively become the vernacular of Europe. Furthermore, while Europe today is by no means a melting pot (the European Union and its Euro notwithstanding), in architecture at least, the modernist credos so forcefully expressed after World War I by the Bauhaus leaders and Le Corbusier, among others, have taken precedence in this century over regional differences.

The architects included in this volume draw upon the whole history of modern architecture. To understand their work, therefore, it is necessary to understand the legacy of modernism that shapes the intellectual and physical context within which they build. Europe may be said to have been the cradle of modernism, if we accept that its emergence as an organized, recognized cultural phenomenon was heralded by the formation of the Bauhaus in Germany in 1919. Surely formal advances in Europe were influenced by news from America, whose technological advances, especially in the form of the skyscraper, and architectural innovations, such as the open plan of Frank Lloyd Wright, were closely studied. Nonetheless, it was in Europe that the sense of release brought on by the end of World War I, with the massive social change that took place at that time, most directly propelled aesthetic advances. The new modern movement represented both a stylistic and social break; it assumed a symbolic role representing a real and emphatic shift in how life was to be lived.

World War II, on the other hand, caused such widespread material and psychological devastation in Europe that the decades after the war were largely dedicated to rebuilding what had been destroyed. Technological progress did continue, in the areas, for example, of prefabrication, high-rise design, thin building skins, and tensile structures; however, in many parts of Europe, especially Germany, this period proved to be a time characterized more by stylistic consolidation than by invention.

It was not until almost a quarter of a century later, with the advent of postmodernism, that stylistic change came to architecture. That movement took an entirely different form in Europe than it did in America. The genesis in both places was the same, for by the late 1960s, it was impossible to ignore the ever-widening discrepancy between the optimistic view of continual progress that lay at the heart of the modern movement and the reality of a world afflicted by the Holocaust, the Cold War, and, in Europe especially, the growing threat of nuclear arms. In America, this intellectual crisis engendered a nostalgic retreat to the premodern past, an approach regarded with skepticism by most European architects. In Europe, on the other hand, it ushered in a time of cynicism and a reevaluation of modernism that continues today, propelled by Rem Koolhaas (page 68) and others.

For the most part, however, the past two decades have been, architecturally speaking, a time of relative tranquillity. Economic growth has opened widespread opportunities for building, opportunities augmented by the fall of the Iron Curtain. Architectural innovation has been spurred on by an embarrassment of riches or, more specifically, by the problems brought on by affluence and the mixed blessings of civilization's advance. Rampant suburban development in Europe as in America, a looming scarcity of building materials and energy sources, and the need to preserve not only endangered landscape but also aging urban fabric and historic structures are some of the broad issues that define architectural practice in Europe, as throughout the developed world, at the end of the twentieth century.

The houses shown in this volume all respond to one or another of these issues. Although a small sampling, they nevertheless provide, on an anecdotal basis, intelligent, responsible, and inspired examples of problem-solving and the ongoing search for an architecture expressive of the age.

. . . HOUSE NOW

This search is conducted in a variety of settings, from urban to rural, with a growing number of hybrid sites in between. There are examples here of new urban residences that respect well-defined city settings, with no compromise to their modernity. In their townhouse designs, for example, both Archea (page 54) and Architecture Studio (page 162) chose to play by the rules that define streetscapes in the town of Leffe, Italy, and the city of Paris respectively; they preserve the urban fabric while inserting an original and clearly modern design. Similar constraints shape a corner house in Tokyo (page 86) by architects Peter Wilson and Julia Bolles-Wilson. Designed through an exchange of fax messages between the architects in Germany and their Japanese client, this project illustrates both the common issues related to building in any late twentieth century city in either hemisphere and the unique conditions of Tokyo. Other architects, building at the edges of cities where agricultural and urban conditions collide, endeavor to bring definition to areas of unplanned ambiguity. These include Cino Zucchi (page 194), who proposes an alternative to the typical suburban villa, and Miralles, Tagliabue (page 46), who incorporate existing semi-agricultural structures into a new and distinctly urban ensemble.

Several of the projects shown grapple with the issue of diminishing resources. Architects Driendl ★ Steixner (page 168) have designed a prototype for an energy-efficient structure, while Jourda Perraudin (page 78) take a more metaphorical approach to the issue of environmental preservation in a house that rests but lightly on the land. Four architects in this volume address the relationship between old and new structures, including Miralles, Tagliabue; Christoph Mäckler (page 184) who has designed an addition to a winery; Barone Pottgiesser (page 116) who have inserted a new construction into an old barn; and Klaus Kada (page 130) who enlarged a Victorian residence. These very different projects have in common a freedom of expression that chooses modern forms to complement and not copy the original, older building.

The language of modernism, in fact, underlies all these efforts to address contemporary concerns. While the houses shown in this volume share the history of modernism, they also represent a striking license in its interpretation and application. Even those architects who reject the modernist label, for example Francine Houben of Mecanoo (page 228), apply its problem-solving methodology. Moreover, these architects have managed to separate modernism from the dogma associated with the style at various points in its evolution. Resisting rigid ideology on the one hand and mindless formal imitation on the other, they search the rich history of modern architecture for the model or mentor best suited to their own personal explorations, or to the specific requirements of the project at hand. All of modern architecture—from the many approaches taken by the ever inventive Le Corbusier to the work of less famous architects such as Pierre Chareau—is available for examination and adaptation. The house in Lyons by Jourda Perraudin, for example, is suggestive of Le Corbusier's lesser-known Maisons Jaoul, while his more celebrated Ronchamp Chapel has inspired several details, including a wall in the house by Vicens•Ramos (page 92). Even Mies van der Rohe, censured for many years as the original source of the cold glass boxes that have spoiled so many cities, is being reexamined. His works, and in particular his early houses, are being recognized for their sensuous elegance and transparency, features that are in some cases reapplied in unusual form, as in the expressionistic Möbius House by Ben van Berkel (page 14). Contributions from the United States and Japan have been added to the mix, as in the Suzuki House (page 86) which is part Tadao Ando, part Le Corbusier, and part MTV.

Moreover, regional variations in the application of modernist principles continue to develop, as they have throughout the history of modernism. A tradition of wood craftsmanship in the Vorarlberg region of Austria, for example, has influenced the otherwise rationalist work of Baumschlager & Eberle (pages 30 and 38). Similarly, the rugged austerity of the house by Herzog & de Meuron (page 124) is uniquely suited to and adapted from the rural traditions of Switzerland and the adjacent regions of northern Italy. Other architects such as Eduardo Souto de Moura (page 176) of Portugal use local building techniques in house designs whose organization is distinctly modern. In neighboring Spain, recent political history and the consequent late flowering of modern architecture have produced a body of work that is classically modern; yet even here, such a generality immediately disintegrates under the weight of individual works that defy easy categorization. One need only compare the very pure and abstract compositions of Alberto Campo Baeza (page 138) to the exuberant expressionism of Lapeña and Torres (page 220) to see the variety sheltered beneath the umbrella of Spanish modernism.

Yet another aspect of modernism—its emphasis on innovative building technology—has evolved over the past three decades into the sub-movement called high tech. Taking root in England, where it evolved to the tremendous level of refinement visible in the work of John Young (page 150), this offshoot celebrates twentieth-century materials and focuses on the perfect design of architectural details. Sustained, though only in part, by the early modernist vision of salvation through technology, high tech endorses an optimistic belief in progress that is anomalous in our times.

Other architects have taken the opposite tack. In severing the language of classic modernism from its original ideology and adopting a distinctly postmodern stance, they use architectural language to question cultural norms and engage issues that confront society at large. Significantly, many of the architects in this volume challenge that most characteristic element of twentieth-century life, the suburb. The almost transcendental purity of Ungers House III (page 108) expresses a resolute aloofness from its suburban setting. Baumschlager & Eberle, in their house in Hard (page 38), call attention to the growing pressures of haphazard urban development on the pristine Austrian countryside. In the Netherlands and Belgium, Van Berkel & Bos (pages 14 and 24) and Xaveer De Geyter (page 214) confront the blight of suburban development, while capitalizing on the irony of building in the very situation their designs critique. In so doing they reflect the influence of Rem Koolhaas (page 68), who advocates the application of an urban sensibility to all architectural projects, and they protest the detrimental effects of typical suburban planning on the environment and on the quality of life itself.

It is to be hoped, then, that these twenty-nine houses are studied not only for their formal beauty, which is self-evident, but for the ideas each examines. Taken together, they suggest a multifaceted vision of European architecture at the end of the twentieth century and a convincing display of the many possibilities inherent in European modernism. ∎

MÖBIUS HOUSE
HET GOOI, THE NETHERLANDS

In the Möbius House, designed by Ben van Berkel, the eponymous geometric form—an endless loop—is a metaphor not only for the architectural design but for the life lived within it. The Möbius strip is defined by the *Random House Dictionary* as "a continuous, one-sided surface formed by twisting one end of a rectangular strip through 180 degrees about the longitudinal axis of the strip and attaching this end to the other." In this house, domestic life is graphed as a continuous line of overlapping social and work life, family and individual life, or, seen another way, a never-ending cycle of sleeping, working, and living. Movement from one activity to the next becomes the generating principle for design.

Second-floor bedrooms jut out over the long, glazed south-facing facade (above), which ends in the dramatically cantilevered studio (top).

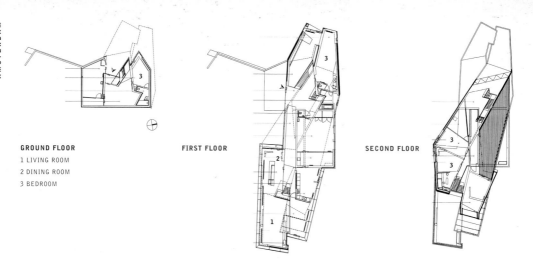

GROUND FLOOR

1 LIVING ROOM
2 DINING ROOM
3 BEDROOM

FIRST FLOOR

SECOND FLOOR

The actual architecture of this 5,500-square-foot house attempts to grant physical reality to this conceptual diagram. Significantly, the heart of the house is not the fireplace, which occupies an extreme corner of the living room, but the stair, center of movement, which marks the fulcrum of rotation in plan. The upper bedroom floor is twisted off the axis of the main living floor, creating a variety of very complex three-dimensional relationships. The two principal materials, glass and concrete, are woven together in their own endless loop, reversing roles and shifting from foreground to background, or metamorphosing from one application to another. Concrete walls become furniture; glass windows become walls.

It is perhaps paradoxical that a design methodology that claims to have little or nothing to do with the traditional, architectural preoccupation with form-giving should produce so distinct and beautiful a form. The model or metaphor of the Möbius strip is admittedly not architectural at all, but its interpretation here in built materials, combined with the integration of indoors and out, and the introduction of natural light make the Möbius House an exceedingly rich, sensuous piece of very physical architecture. Details such as the subtly decorative patterning left by formwork on the concrete walls or the corner window connecting two second-floor bedrooms show a mastery of traditional architectural detailing that goes well beyond the diagram. Both the house and the diagram upon which it is based are made possible by the use of the computer, which has allowed this exploration of complex, so-called topological geometries in architecture.

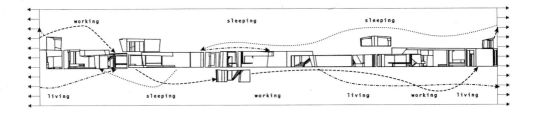

The architects' interpretation of the Möbius strip (above) results in interiors of rich spatial and material complexity (facing page).

Seen here from three different viewpoints, the stair is the fulcrum of the house and the point around which the design revolves.

The built-in shelves (facing page) are used to define architectural space. The photos on this page document details of the house, such as the fireplace (top), in a cinematic fashion.

Like many of the architects whose work is shown in this volume, van Berkel and his partner Caroline Bos are not entirely comfortable with the label "modernist" and the legacy it connotes. As if to dramatize their commitment to an architecture that is not about autonomous object-making but about process and movement, the Möbius House was photographed not only in the typical style of architectural photography but cinematically, with actors whose presence simulates the sense of movement through space in time. In their recent monograph, *Move*, the architects, who are known for a number of significant public commissions including Rotterdam's Erasmus Bridge, present "a manifesto against modernism, which is still based on techniques of fragmentation and collage." They argue instead for an architecture of "inclusiveness" or "connectivity," as symbolized by the Möbius strip, and they have opened a new office based on this principle. The United Net (UN) Studio, which operates as an adjunct to their architectural practice, proposes an interdisciplinary approach to design that melds science, engineering, computers, media, interior and landscape design, building consulting, and photography into one continuous loop. ■

The tight skin of the facade (above) becomes transparent at night, revealing the house's inner complexity (facing page).

VILLA WILBRINK
AMERSFOORT, THE NETHERLANDS

All architecture is best understood in the context of the time and place for which it was designed—the society that surrounded it, the philosophical ideas that predominated at the time, and the state of the built environment. This truism is especially valid for those works that seek to critique the world around them. In other words, to understand the revolutionary, first examine the status quo.

To understand Villa Wilbrink, a single-family house designed by Ben van Berkel for a new subdivision in the city of Amersfoort, one must study its suburban context. This brooding "bunker," as the architect calls it, launches a scathing attack on middle-class Dutch suburbia. Even the name Villa Wilbrink mocks the aspirations of the typical Dutch bourgeois homeowner, whose every dearly held value is challenged here. The house quite literally turns its back upon its neighbors, a collection of architect-designed houses on streets named for famous architects of history, including Le Corbusier, Pier Luigi Nervi, and Baron Haussmann. (Villa Wilbrink is on Aaltostraat.) The entrance is skewed and the house itself hidden from street view by the garage; the driveway meets the street at an arbitrary, even awkward, angle. The glazed brick of the facades has been laid with minimal mortar so that the surfaces congeal into a smooth, monolithic box, as seemingly impenetrable as it is imposing. The bedroom windows are hooded; the living room windows are set at grade level. Indeed, the house has been described by one critic as appearing to rise from the earth like some sort of geological form, forced to the surface by a cataclysmic event.

The Wilbrink House presents a fortresslike exterior to the street (facing page). The entrance is concealed in the inner courtyard behind the garage (above).

The "garden" was designed for a client who reportedly hates his country's national pastime. The front "yard" is an inclined plane covered with asphalt; the back garden is an abstract grid of trees "mulched" in gravel. Instead of minimizing the footprint and maximizing open space, the single-story, 2,000-square-foot house spreads out to consume its plot. Bourgeois this house is not.

Floor-to-ceiling windows in the living room (facing page) open to the rear garden or the inner courtyard (above). The corner window (top) is set at grade to preserve privacy while admitting light.

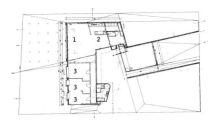

1 LIVING ROOM
2 DINING ROOM
3 BEDROOM

Yet once the walls of this fortress are breached, the house inside is surprisingly peaceful and protected, its simple plan disingenuously functional in nature. The architects have graduated to more complex, three-dimensional modeling for more recent designs such as the Möbius House (page 14). Wilbrink, however, presages the use of movement as the generating principle for architecture that is evident in the later Möbius project. The plan here moves with its occupants in a curve from the entrance past a half-bath and kitchen and through the living/dining space to the bedrooms, which are lined up along a simple glazed corridor. This procession around its edges shapes a central courtyard; the form, however, is left open and incomplete; space is contained, but only briefly.

The simplicity and seeming casualness of the plan contrast with the careful, precise detailing of materials, as in the curved wood-slat overhang that protects glazed walls lining the courtyard, or the simple kitchen window that looks out on a gravel garden. These details humanize a house that seeks to meet the needs of its occupants within a manifesto denouncing the limitations of twentieth-century suburbia. ∎

The rear facade shows the monolithic treatment of the brick wall, laid with minimal mortar (above), through which the boxed bedroom windows project (facing page).

KERN HOUSE
LOCHAU, AUSTRIA

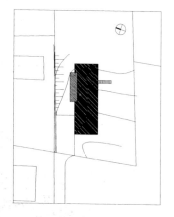

"With every utopia or vision, the reality remains the most important moment. We won't be able to do away with reality." This statement by Carlo Baumschlager reflects the starting point for his designs and those of his partner, Dieter Eberle. They design elegantly and with vision, as even a cursory glance at their two houses shown in this book reveals (see also the Häusler House, page 38). Yet *how* they build ostensibly interests them more than *what* they build. When they discuss their work, they talk about function and budget, letting the form speak for itself.

Both Baumschlager and Eberle studied in Vienna, but in the mid-1970s each returned to his roots in the Vorarlberg to work. In this westernmost state of Austria, with its beautiful natural attractions including Lake Constance, the Bregenz woods, and the Arlberg mountains, the two became part of a group of builders, architects, and artists who strove to combine local traditions and modern technology while bucking the established architectural authorities. In the hippie spirit of the times, the Vorarlberg group members worked cooperatively, sharing experiences, skills, and clients, building economically, ecologically, and attractively. Their philosophies and methods stemmed from two divergent sets of teaching: the rationalist approach taught in the 1960s at the Vienna Academy of Fine Arts, and the example of a local carpenter/engineer, Rudolf Waeger, who created simple, beautifully detailed buildings of wood.

The house, a glass box surrounded by an outer skin of wood louvers, is relatively open to its surroundings on its south side (facing page), where the main entrance is placed, and its west facade (above), which embraces a loggia with spectacular views of Lake Constance.

The seamless metal staircase contrasts with the wood louvers, which are set vertical at the base of the building and are increasingly angled toward the top of the building.

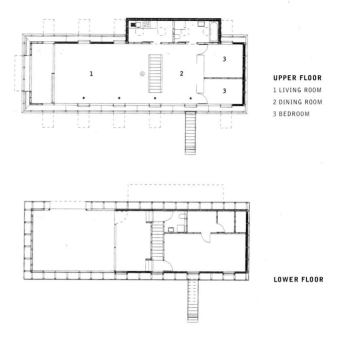

UPPER FLOOR
1 LIVING ROOM
2 DINING ROOM
3 BEDROOM

LOWER FLOOR

33

These influences are still unmistakable in the work of Baumschlager and Eberle, who began working together in 1985. Their pure built forms meet the landscape simply; they use wood in ways that are both traditional and original; and economy of time and money is an important starting point for them. They make extensive use of the computer, and over the years have developed a database system that can quickly coordinate building form, building method, details, and cost. They do not refrain from repeating a detail in project after project, wherever they consider its use appropriate. In their ability to merge beauty, stability, and function, they are successful at referring to their regional roots while moving toward the future.

The Kern residence sits lightly on its gently sloping site, a wood cage sheltering a glass box within. The glass box seems to reach out through the wood sheath to touch the ground ever so slightly by means of a metal staircase, like a ship temporarily docked or an airplane on the landing field. Through the use of the inner and outer boxes, the 1,000-square-foot house combines the advantages of glass (abundant views from inside outward) with the benefits of wood louvers (sunscreening, privacy, and a warm appearance).

The regularly spaced louvers lie flat against the structure at the base of the house and are increasingly angled toward the roof. In this way, the view from outside is limited: standing beside the house, one cannot see directly into the uninteresting areas on the lower level (garage, storage) and can perceive little more than the upper story's ceiling and, at night, the glow of lamplight. The louvers thus appear denser at the base and lighter at the top. This simple arrangement produces a number of interesting effects. The graduated angles of the outer shell's horizontal louvers create a crescendo, while the rhythmic spacing of the vertical structural dividers in the inner shell forms their counterpoint. The inner box, in its glassiness, is clear, hard, and modern, while the protective outer shell, in its woodsiness, is soft, diffuse, almost filigreed, and relatively traditional in appearance. The modern/traditional contrast relates, in fact, to the methods of production: the inner glass box, which is set back 20 inches from the wood screen to allow for cleaning (a catwalk is provided at the second story), was erected in a week using prefabricated panels, while the outer grid was custom-produced on site.

The upper story serves as the main living area, with bedrooms for the client (a single mother and her daughter) at the east end, a living room and screened loggia overlooking Lake Constance at the other end, and a cantilevered, shingle-clad box holding kitchen and bathroom along the north side. Garage, storage, and an additional bedroom/study occupy the lower level. ∎

The outer box of wood louvers is separated from the inner wall, and a catwalk between them allows for maintenance of both skins (facing page). The louvers are interrupted to provide open views from the main living space (above), which at night glows like a lantern (following pages).

BAUMSCHLAGER & EBERLE ARCHITECTURE OFFICE
LOCHAU, AUSTRIA

HÄUSLER HOUSE
HARD, AUSTRIA

Given the natural beauty of the Vorarlberg area of Austria, it is not surprising that the valleys are subjected to enormous development pressures. In these areas, the population density reaches urban levels, though the infrastructure is inadequate; traffic congestion, for example, has become the norm. For this reason, Baumschlager and Eberle do not always depict the meeting of past and present traditions in a gentle fashion, as they did in their Kern House (page 30). Sometimes, as in the Häusler House shown here, the encounter is interpreted trenchantly.

The 2,200-square-foot Häusler House, like the Kern House, is made up of clearly differentiated inner and outer rectangular shells, but the Häusler House is both more complex spatially and tougher in its materials and form. This more aggressive stance is surely a reaction to its location, a no-man's-land neither quite urban nor totally rural. Stand-offish toward the outside world, the house focuses inward on the gentle domestic realm; even its open-air spaces are strictly defined as terraces within the gridded zone.

The structure's concrete skin is sparsely fenestrated on three sides, but on the fourth side, the concrete wall is broken up into a grid of columns (above). The house is entered through a passageway hollowed out of the body of the building (top). The wooden garden shed stands behind the concrete house (following pages).

LOWER FLOOR
1 LIVING ROOM
2 DINING ROOM
3 BEDROOM

UPPER FLOOR

The two-story living room (above and facing page) is traversed by a mezzanine bridge that connects the children's and parents' bedrooms.

The exterior shell is of concrete, while the inner, more complex volume is clad in wood, as if a gentle creature is being harbored within a brusque carapace. The concrete case consists of three sparsely fenestrated walls, with the fourth wall broken up into a grid of columns, two levels of twelve bays each. Off-center along the rectangle's long side, a two-bay-wide, one-story-high rectangular wood box is "pushed out" to form a garden shed on the land, the only intervention beyond the confines of the concrete box. On either side of the tunnel left by the displaced box are entrance doors, one leading to a one-story rental apartment, the other to the two-story main house. The ground floor of the main house holds the living room, kitchen, dining room, and a two-story outdoor terrace, while the upper floor contains three bedrooms, a large dressing room, and another outdoor terrace, all within the perimeter of the concrete shell. As in the Kern House, wood louvers modulate the direct rays of the sun.

From the inside, the view focuses southward to the mountains. But this is carved up by the concrete grid and doled out, as if even the landscape, increasingly compromised by advancing civilization, is suspect. ∎

Two wood-paneled terraces, including a double-height one beside the living room (left), occur within the house's perimeter.

CASA **LA CLOTA**

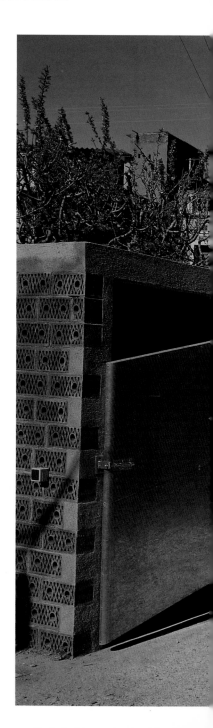

La Clota is typical of the type of city landscape that urban designers like to call "fringe." Situated on the edge of Barcelona in a no-man's-land bordered by agricultural tracts, the semi-industrial district is being slowly transformed into a newly desirable residential neighborhood. Its original houses, many built by their occupants, combined work and home, with workshops on the ground floor and living space above. Some of the houses stood vacant for years, until the pressures of urban development and the construction of a vast park nearby for the Barcelona Olympics combined to give this rather eclectic neighborhood new cachet.

Architect Enric Miralles was no doubt familiar with the area, having completed his renowned archery building in the Olympic Park in 1991. This house in La Clota, designed with partner Benedetta Tagliabue, combines two tiny houses into one 1,200-square-foot whole. The original interiors were cut up into small, dark rooms. The architects responded to this condition with the boldest possible gesture, cutting floors away to create a double-height light well of a library that occupies half of the new house. The openness and even grandeur of this space, its light and height, are completely unexpected and unannounced on the new entrance facade. The walls here were so corroded that the architects decided to build self-supporting library shelves inserted into the old frame. Original beams are exposed and

The conversion of a pair of owner-built houses into a single unit in a light industrial/agricultural district preserves much of the homes' original character, as seen in this entrance courtyard.

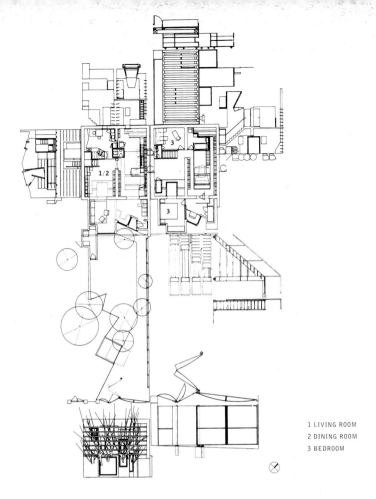

1 LIVING ROOM
2 DINING ROOM
3 BEDROOM

painted in white stripes that accentuate the juxtaposition of old and new. Past and present coexist as separate but equal parts of a new whole. "Being modern doesn't mean you have to destroy the past, any more than being historicist means you only save the past," argues Tagliabue.

One enters the house through a long court bordered on one side by a crumbling wall. No attempt has been made to "beautify" this gritty edge, which shapes the project's aesthetic. The front addition, which contains the entrance hall on the ground floor and a study and bedroom above, sits behind a new facade of irregular outline that continues the original pattern of concrete frame and brick infill. Inside, a fragment of the original balcony railing marks the edge between new and old. Pitched roofs have been removed and new windows installed, their simple wood frames inset into the surrounding brick so that the elements remain distinct.

The composite plan (above) shows both the ground floor (left half) and upper floor, together with elevations and sections. A narrow addition to the front of the existing building contains the entrance hall and living room (seen through window, facing page).

The new facade's irregular profile creates interesting interior spaces (above). Elements of the old house have been retained and enhanced for emphasis; these include beams (facing page, top) and a balustrade (visible at the bottom of the photo, facing page, bottom).

While thoroughly modern, the house exemplifies an ongoing tradition of craftsmanship in Barcelona. Miralles and Tagliabue acknowledge the influence of early Catalan modernists Antonio Gaudí and Josep María Jujol, not in any imitation of the very personal and even idiosyncratic styles of these precursors but in a continued emphasis on craft and technique in architecture. The small size of their firm, like many in Barcelona, allows an unusually close collaboration with plasterers, metalworkers, furniture makers, and other fabricators in the production of an architecture that is strongly material in nature. ∎

The second floor has been cut away to create a double-height library (facing page) lit by a dramatic sculptural skylight (above).

STUDIO ARCHEA ASSOCIATES
FLORENCE

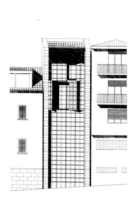 

Laura Andreini, Marco Casamonti, and Giovanni Polazzi opened Studio Archea Associates (their "laboratory of architecture") in 1988 with the purpose of using real design projects as opportunities for experimentation. Through their research, as they explain in the book *Young Italian Architects* (Birkhäuser, 1998), they aim to discover new uses for traditional materials and new expressions for classical and vernacular forms. They are also interested in finding fresh ways to incorporate a medieval randomness in design composition and new means to impart a sense of belonging and immortality. These goals have become recurrent themes in their work, as seen in commissions for buildings as large as a recreation center in Bergamo and as small as the row house, shown here, in the town of Leffe in Val Seriana.

The demolition of an existing building in Leffe's historic center left an odd-shaped lot fronting on two streets. On the main street, the lot width is a mere 17 feet, while on the minor street, the lot jogs to provide space for a 32-foot facade. The wider frontage, however, was encumbered by strict restraints. Because of the proximity of the windows on the adjacent structures, the building had to be set back following a precisely prescribed irregular line. For convenience, the architects placed both the main entrance door and the garage entry to the 2,600-square-foot house on the minor street. The living and dining rooms on the lower two floors and the master bedroom on the top floor are located adjacent to the main street in order to take advantage of the dramatic valley views. In the most awkward of the volumes created by the jagged perimeter, the architects incorporated the stair tower for the four-story house.

On the street side of this townhouse, slatted shutters made of copper and steel cover the fully glazed facade (above and facing page). Closed, the shutters ensure privacy; open, they offer views down to the valley.

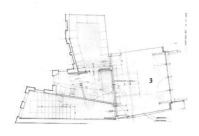

THIRD FLOOR

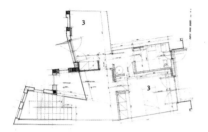

SECOND FLOOR

FIRST FLOOR

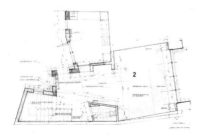

GROUND FLOOR
1 LIVING ROOM
2 DINING ROOM
3 BEDROOM

An open staircase and a three-story-high opening between floors (above and facing page) lend the space an expansive feeling despite the house's relatively constricted perimeter.

The architects have not been limited by these constraints; quite the contrary. They could conceivably have achieved a more regular, continuous building facade on the alley by slightly reducing the size of the house. Instead, they followed the perimeter exactly, thereby realizing their desired goal of medieval randomness. They found a novel way to introduce light into this facade, and in doing so managed to recall certain vernacular forms: instead of using traditional windows, which were restricted because of the nearby houses, they introduced small, regularly spaced slits into the masonry wall to permit beams of light to enter the building, as in a hayloft or a barn.

"Invention," write the architects, ". . . does not consist in the choice of materials but in its modes of use." Reflecting this interest in varied applications of materials, they employed Santa Fiora stone on the alley facade to impart a sense of tradition and immortality, while designing an unusual copper-lined overhang at the roofline. On the main street side, copper is used again, here in a particularly inventive way. This elevation is largely glazed to allow fine views down to the valley, but to ensure privacy on the relatively narrow street, the architects devised a system of operable shutters. These shutters, pierced by regularly spaced slits that repeat the rhythm of the house's stone facade on the alley, are made of stainless steel and oxidized copper, the latter choice reflecting another favorite subtheme of the architects, the application of naturally weathering materials. Here again, the materials are familiar, but their employment is truly inventive. ■

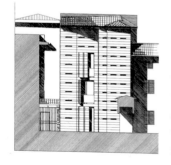

The angled walls on the alley (above and facing page) convey the impression of a medieval fortress. Faced in stone that is pierced by horizontal slits, this facade has one bank of shutters that matches those on the street wall.

ALONSO-PLANAS HOUSE
ESPLUGUES DE LLOBREGAT, BARCELONA

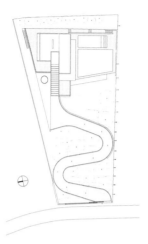

This dramatic white house stands confidently atop its steep site. Its louvered windows focus both west down the mountain and south across the width of its long, trapezoidal lot, capturing views of two valleys, the city of Barcelona, and the sea in the distance. The house's low wings—one containing an almost-buried painting and sculpture studio lit by a strip of sloping clerestory windows, the other the tunnel leading toward the entrance—extend to embrace oncoming visitors as they make their way along a winding path up to the house.

Above its base, which is dug into the mountain and stretches the width of the site, the 8,000-square-foot house rises three stories. These three stories are contained in a long and narrow mass that runs perpendicular to the contour lines. This mass, in fact, is made up of thin overlapping rectilinear volumes with windows facing down or across the site. The master bedroom faces west, down the slope, its relatively narrow bank of windows protected by aluminum louvers. The family/living room volume faces south, across the site, with wide, louvered windows overlooking the swimming pool and the grassy patio atop the art studio. The family room on the first level of this volume opens to the patio, while its upper stories accommodate a two-story living room with a mezzanine library. Behind the

Aluminum louvers shade the windows that face down and across the sloping site (above and following pages).
The base of the building incorporates a skylit tunnel into the house (top) and an underground art atelier, which is lit by a
sloping band of clerestory windows.

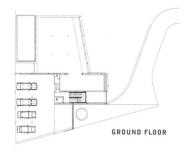

GROUND FLOOR

living room is the children's bedroom wing, with access to terraces on the house's north side. Walls are faced in white engineer's brick, and aluminum louvers are suspended and held taut by a system of steel wires.

Carlos Ferrater has designed a wide variety of projects over the past two decades, among them office buildings, schools, parks (including the New Botanical Garden of Barcelona), and convention centers, for which, wrote architectural historian William Curtis recently, "Ferrater has evolved a corresponding spectrum of responses." For his houses, noted Curtis, Ferrater's response entails "entering into dialogue with the forces of landscape, sun, and sea."

The Alonso-Planas House suggests a number of connections to modernist models. The massing of its white cubic forms, the horizontal thrust of its great louvered windows, and its glamorous sense of style are reminiscent of the work of that master of sophisticated hauteur, the French art deco architect Robert Mallet-Stevens. The impression the house conveys of strict cleanliness combined with hedonism suggests Richard Neutra's 1928 Lovell House. Finally, the work of a more recent modernist and a fellow countryman, Josep Lluis Sert, is recalled in the playing of windowed volumes, pinwheel fashion, against a solid service volume. But in the end, the main accomplishment of this design is the distillation of modernist ideas to reflect and celebrate the bright Mediterranean light. ∎

FIRST FLOOR
1 LIVING ROOM
2 DINING ROOM
3 BEDROOM

SECOND FLOOR

THIRD FLOOR

Stairs lead up from the two-story living room (above) to a mezzanine library. The living room overlooks both the patio, which stands atop the art atelier (facing page), and the swimming pool (following pages).

Rem Koolhaas (with Madelon Vriesendorp and Elia and Zoe Zenghelis) founded the Office of Metropolitan Architecture in 1975 to practice and promulgate a particular approach to design. This approach is based upon two Koolhaas passions: an enthusiasm for the twentieth-century metropolis as a vital, self-propagating organism and an intense interest in the heroic period of modern architecture. To elucidate and expand upon these two concerns, Koolhaas, who began his working life as a screenplay writer, weaves elaborate allegorical narratives around them. He then gives these stories vivid physical form that he further manipulates by using, among other artistic means, fragmentation and collage. O.M.A. has been involved in numerous prominent projects and competitions, including two designs for Lille, France: the Euralille urban master plan and the design of the Congrexpo. But his ideas have been disseminated most especially through his publications. In *S,M,L,XL,* his 1995 book about his architectural fantasies and experiences, and in his beautifully illustrated 1978 book, *Delirious New York,* he inspires his readers to sense the potency of urban scale and energy. This vitality invigorates even the smallest of his projects, as is patently clear from the Villa dall'Ava, shown here.

On its street side, the Villa dall'Ava rises three stories above the ground (left and above) behind a preexisting wall along the sidewalk.

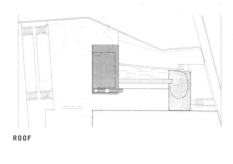

ROOF

SECOND FLOOR

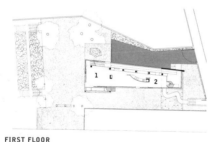

FIRST FLOOR
1 LIVING ROOM
2 DINING ROOM
3 BEDROOM

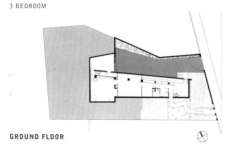

GROUND FLOOR

In *S,M,L,XL* Koolhaas describes the challenges intrin
in this relatively small commission for the design of a tw
bedroom, 3,500-square-foot house. Among the intimidati
factors, explains the architect, were the clients' anticipati
of a "masterpiece," as well as the presence of two villas by
Corbusier nearby (one of them the Villa Savoye). Amo
the complicating conditions were exacting and comp
zoning laws and conservative neighbors who delayed t
execution of Koolhaas's bold design. And among the ch
lenging elements was the need to satisfy both the husban
wish for a glass house and the wife's desire for a rooftop p
with views of the distant Eiffel Tower, forcing the archit
to resolve the problem of supporting the weight of the p
on a glass structure.

The resultant house is a buildup of volumes layer
both horizontally and vertically. The top-to-bottom co
position, reminiscent of Mies van der Rohe's 19
Tugendhat House, captures a glass house between a so
plinth below (in dall'Ava's case a slate-faced entrance lev
and the bedroom level above. The front-to-back organi
zation finds two aluminum-clad bedroom aeries hoveri
in the air like tree houses, separated by the long lap p
from which one indeed catches views of Paris's legenda
tower. The above-ground location, wide proportions, a
horizontal strip windows of the bedroom wings recall
Corbusier's Villa Savoye, as do the multiple means to asce
through the house: stairways at the back and the front co
necting the three floor levels, and a shallow ramp leadi
from the entrance to the living room.

The daughter's bedroom suite, encased in corrugated aluminum, is supported by slim pipe columns (facing page).
The pipe columns, tilted at various angles, surround the path to the entrance hall, which is clad in slate.

EAST—WEST SECTION

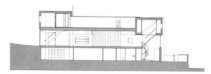

WEST—EAST SECTION

SOUTH—NORTH SECTION

The living room (left), which can be separated from the library by silk drapes and screened from the outside by a bamboo curtain, can be reached by a ramp along one side of the house (above). The kitchen (top) is enclosed in a curved wall of corrugated polyester resin.

Much of the immediate charm of the house lies in Koolhaas's choice of colors and materials. The main floor's glass walls are alternately clear and etched, with screens of bamboo, perforated metal, and yellow silk, which can be drawn to create an atmosphere of intimacy. A curved wall of translucent corrugated polyester resin encloses the kitchen, plywood encases the library storage wall, and random perforations dot the plaster ceiling of the living area. The wedge shape of the main body of the house (the result of zoning regulations) creates forced perspectives, which Koolhaas intensifies or purposely contradicts by various means. To diminish the perceived distance from the front of the house to the back, the corrugations of the rear bedroom pavilion are finished in copper and are wider than those of the front pavilion. Similarly, the slim, randomly canted pipe columns around the house's entrance are graded in color from white to black, once again, notes Koolhaas, to counteract the effect of perspective.

Facing the garden to the rear, the house rises two stories above the ground (above). The upper story, a copper-finished aluminum volume containing the master bedroom suite, recalls in its proportions Le Corbusier's Villa Savoye.

But what most inspires wonder is the sleight of hand employed in the structure of the house. The cantilever of the master bedroom pavilion seems to be impossibly long and appears to spring from a glass wall; the pipe columns supporting the daughter's bedroom appear to be merely decorative; and the rooftop pool seems to be borne by the glass alone, since the actual support—a concrete wall beside the driveway, columns absorbed in the storage wall, and chimney structures—is scarcely perceived. Koolhaas's well-publicized Bordeaux house, like the Villa dall'Ava a three-story scheme with a half-buried ground floor, glazed main floor, and enclosed bedroom floor, also makes a show of structural gymnastics, but in a more aggressive fashion. The Villa dall'Ava is its coquettish counterpart: gracefully acrobatic, colorful, and charming. ■

The clients achieved their desires in the Villa dall'Ava: a glass house encasing the main floor; a rooftop pool with the Eiffel Tower as a distant spectacle (facing page and above); and an unusual piece of architecture.

JOURDA PERRAUDIN, ARCHITECTS
LYONS, FRANCE

HOUSE IN VAISE LYONS, FRANCE

Françoise-Hélène Jourda and Gilles Perraudin worked as a husband-and-wife architectural team during the 1980s and early '90s. During these years, they were known for work that applied the logic of natural phenomena to the development of rational architectural systems. That is, they designed basic building units (structural elements and spatial configurations) that responded eloquently to the problems at hand and could be repeated for economy and harmony. The School of Architecture in Lyons, completed in 1988, is a case in point, as is their own family residence, shown here. Both employ repetitive bays and standardized structural parts, as well as integrated overhead canopies that mimic the shading function of a forest's canopy.

The house, furthermore, represents most expressively the couple's philosophy of designing only that which is essential. Incorporated within this concept is the desire to minimize a structure's impact upon the earth: it should be, they feel, both materially and spiritually lightweight and even transient. Their 1,700-square-foot plywood dwelling, built adjacent to their work studio within the walled lot of a former presbytery, barely skims the surface of the ground and has the feel of a temporary encampment.

The long, glass-fronted house (left), built of plywood sandwich panels on a prefabricated steel frame, is shaded by a large fabric canopy (above).

1 LIVING ROOM
2 DINING ROOM
3 BEDROOM

The house's prefabricated steel structure—posts, beams, and a light frame for the canopy—was assembled on site in a matter of days to form an eight-bay skeleton, each bay measuring 10 by 24 feet in plan. Polyester fabric was stretched over the frame within a day, providing a shelter under which the box of the house was installed. Sandwich panels, consisting of plywood skins separated by wood stiffeners and filled with insulation, make up the floor, which sits on steel beams a foot above the ground, as well as the ceiling, which hangs from the roof beams. Similar sandwich panels are used for the walls on the east, north, and west sides, while the long south wall is formed of sliding glass panels lined by interior louvered blinds. These glass doors open onto a large deck, itself shaded by the canopy. Shallow plywood barrel vaults confer distinction upon the third and fourth bays, which serve as living/dining room.

The two bays that serve as living/dining space are roofed with plywood barrel vaults.

The open bay system allows for a great deal of flexibility. Bathrooms are kept to a zone along the north wall, a zone that includes alcoves that can be separated from the main space by means of sliding fabric panels. The kitchen is a free-standing island within the living/dining area, while bedrooms were conceived as tiny enclosed pods, each just big enough for a bed and a night table. One double pod was designed to stand within the western bay and serve as the master bedroom, and three single pods in the eastern bays were designed for the children. The adaptable nature of the design—one of the architects' aims—was recently put to the test, as a second floor consisting of high plywood barrel vaults was added above the original bedroom bays to provide more generous space for the children's bedrooms.

The building's repetitive bays and standardized structural elements make a cogent case for industrialized housing, even on a small scale. Furthermore, with its shallow, sturdily proportioned vaults, the house is reminiscent of Le Corbusier's 1951 Maisons Jaoul, which were also designed with economy and ease of construction in mind. Here, however, the architects wished to call upon a minimum of the earth's resources, building a structure that is light in fact and in appearance. The delicate linearity of the steel members is juxtaposed against the taut surfaces of fabric and plywood, while the canopy hovers like a butterfly over the long, simple box. ∎

*An alcove at the back of the living/dining room (above and facing page) can be screened off from the main space
by means of a sliding fabric panel.*

The glass wall on the south side of the house opens out to a deck, shaded by the canopy, along the length of the building (above and facing page).

BOLLES + WILSON ARCHITECTURE OFFICE
MÜNSTER, GERMANY

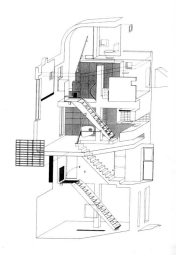

Designed in a series of faxes between an Australian architect working in Germany and his Japanese client, the Suzuki House is a witty commentary on many aspects of late-twentieth-century urban life. Sites for single-family houses are scarce in Tokyo—a corner lot rarer still—and the tiny dimensions of this 18-by-23-foot plot enforce a kind of miniaturization or, as the architects call it, a compression of elements. Four tightly packed and stacked floors—one a basement studio—meet the needs of a small nuclear family. The street-level parking space beneath the house is perfectly sized for the family Mini. The children's bedroom and parents' sleeping balcony are suspended above the double-height living/dining room, which gains thereby an illusion of openness far grander than its footprint suggests.

A day view of the house reveals its relationship to more typical Tokyo neighbors (above),
while at night, the facade takes on the character of a television screen and monitor (facing page).

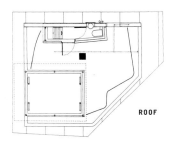

ROOF

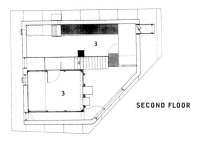

SECOND FLOOR

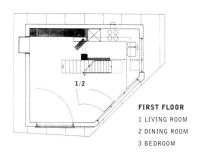

FIRST FLOOR

1 LIVING ROOM
2 DINING ROOM
3 BEDROOM

GROUND FLOOR

A steel stair leads from the main living space to sleeping areas (facing page). Every element of this tiny house has been exquisitely and sometimes playfully detailed, as is the folded wall (top) and stacked cupboards (above).

Although this design might be categorized as a European export, Peter Wilson is no stranger to Japan. He was even fortunate enough as a child to visit Frank Lloyd Wright's Imperial Hotel, since destroyed. His client Arika Suzuki edits an avant-garde Japanese architecture magazine. The 900-square-foot house's elegant and intricately planned interior is all one might expect from such pedigrees. Similarly, elements such as the steel and wood stair or the punched-metal entrance wall are handled in a way that emphasizes what Wilson and his partner, German-born Julia Bolles-Wilson, call the "materiality" of architecture—its "silent qualities" such as "the woodness of wood, the mass of brick, the homogeneity of concrete, the coldness of steel, even the translucence of thin plastic." These qualities have long preoccupied native Japanese modernists such as Tadao Ando, reflecting in turn the influence of Le Corbusier in a give-and-take between East and West that Wilson and his client surely appreciate.

As complex as these influences are, Wilson's touch is exceedingly light. The delightful street facade leaves "high design" to one side altogether in a composition that is pure pop culture, from the splayed, earthquake-resistant "legs" to the wavy banister of a Corbusian roof terrace. Like a huge television or video screen, complete with corner monitor, the facade manages both to protect and project the private family life within. In this corner composition, Wilson has captured urban life in this fascinating city as perhaps only an outsider can; his delicate balance of high design and pop culture, of private and public life, of chaos and calmness defines Tokyo itself. ∎

The bedroom is cantilevered into the living space (above), whose double-height volume and large window shape a space that feels larger than its dimensions suggest (facing page).

VICENS • RAMOS ARCHITECTS
MADRID

HOUSE IN LAS MATAS MADRID

It is something of a cliché in Spain to contrast the more organic, expressionistic architecture of Barcelona with the abstract, rational work of Madrid. In any case, the two schools are united by a common interest in the sculptural aspects of architectural composition, be it organic or cubist. The latter aesthetic is very much in evidence in the House in Las Matas, designed by architects Ignacio Vicens y Hualde and José Antonio Ramos Abengózar.

Taking full advantage of a relatively simple program and an unusually large, open plot, the architects have designed a free composition of abstract, intersecting volumes and planes set down like a cubist pinwheel in the landscape. It is tempting to imagine this to be the house De Stijl master Gerrit Rietveld might have designed had he had so vast and open a site. The composition of overlapping rectangular volumes anchored by a perfect cube is as much sculpture as it is architecture; it stands free of the conventional clues of domestic habitation that typically convey scale and use.

A first view of the house upon approach communicates little of its scale or organization, emphasizing instead its cubist sculptural qualities (left and above).

At the same time, the 8,570-square-foot house neatly resolves the only stipulation given the architects by their clients: that the parents' rooms be separated from those of their six children. That simple goal is enforced not only in plan but also in section. The children's bedrooms are collected in a long, low bar building half buried in the landscape. The entrance to the house is between this rectangular volume and a second one containing the garage and family and dining rooms. Where these two single-story elements overlap, a third, perpendicular volume steps up and over them, culminating in a two-story living room open to the landscape. The master bedroom suite and a catwalk to the mother's office appear to be suspended in this two-story space. The family room nestled beneath the master suite is separated from the double-height living space by a pierced wall. Inset, backlit niches, used for the display of ceramic pieces, pay direct homage to that most sculptural of modern icons, Le Corbusier's chapel at Ronchamp.

Le Corbusier is not the only modern master whose work has influenced Vicens and Ramos. The architects cite Adolf Loos as specific inspiration for the mother's study at Las Matas, which, like the sitting room in Loos's 1928 Moller House, is suspended in the front hall, with views of both the entrance and the yard. But it is the cubist perfectionism of the house that most visitors note. American architect Charles Gwathmey, for example, upon visiting the house, observed that the spaces within were so pure, abstract, and "spiritual" in nature that ordinary furniture appeared intrusive.

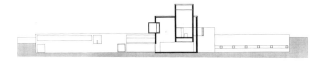

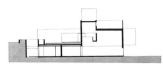

The rear lawn is bounded by the long bar that houses the garage and recreation room and by the cube containing the living room and master suite (facing page). Contrasting colors and materials highlight sculptural projections (above).

The house interior is relatively complex in spatial terms, with ramps connecting levels and half-levels (facing page, bottom) and a catwalk that overlooks the living room connecting to the mother's study (above). The same palette of materials continues in the bathroom (facing page, top).

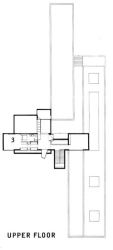

97

At the same time, this "timeless," eternally modern composition of "perfect" forms is clad in imperfect, changeable materials that the architects describe as withstanding the passage of time by changing with time. Larger volumes are clad in rendered concrete that has been stained with iron sulfate to give texture and color. Smaller protruding volumes—the study, office, and master bedroom—are clad in oxidized steel that will continue to rust and darken over the years. Other details—such as the introduction of little courtyards between bedrooms in the children's wing and a careful attention to natural daylight throughout the house—carve an exceedingly livable home out of an uncompromisingly formal composition. ∎

The open, double-height living room and the more sheltered family room (seen left and right, facing page) are treated as one continuous space, separated by an interior wall with a connecting window (top). The family room's copper-clad rear wall is carved in niches, reminiscent of Le Corbusier's chapel at Ronchamp (above). As seen from the rear lawn, the long expanse of the house is anchored by the central living room pavilion (following pages).

O. M. UNGERS, ARCHITECT
COLOGNE, GERMANY

CUBE HOUSE
COLOGNE, GERMANY

The Cube House, which harbors architect Oswald Matthias Ungers' extensive private collection of first-edition architecture books, was added in 1989 to the structure the architect had built for himself in 1958. Both the original building (which initially was his office and residence and now serves only as his office) and its strongly contrasting addition provide important insights into the development of one of Germany's most prominent architectural thinkers of this half-century.

Since his early years as an architect in the 1950s, Ungers has made clear his belief in the autonomy of architecture as a "free" art, as opposed to one of limitations. It is his opinion, in opposition to modernist dogma, that function can adapt to the given building form. For this reason, the transmission of spiritual values has always been for him more important than the fulfillment of the particular function, and the search for architecture's pure, Platonic form has been one of his principal missions. Among the sources he examines to uncover architecture's spiritual content is history, though he does not use history in an imitative sense but rather in an existential one. The resultant forms are always abstract.

A basalt-faced cube, functioning as the architect's library, and a court (right) were added beside the architect's own office, which he designed in the 1950s (above). The ensemble is intended to represent a city in microcosm.

Despite the unity of their underlying themes, Ungers' early works appear quite different from his later designs. The architect's work in the 1950s, of which this Belvederestrasse building is a landmark, has been categorized as "New Brutalist" by architectural historian Reyner Banham and others. Rough red brick and concrete convey a strong sense of materiality, while abstract forms impart an insistent cubist sensibility. With relatively small windows on the street facades, the building appears closed and inwardly focused.

During the 1960s and '70s, Ungers built little but taught and served as department chair at Cornell University and in Berlin and entered numerous large-scale competitions. During this time, he explored ideas of rationalism and investigated ways to integrate contextualism into urban design, always in abstract form. The Cube House and its adjacent garden, conceived during the 1980s, reveal the fruit of these investigations: simple and abstract in its essential parts, its spaces incorporate surprisingly labyrinthine passageways, niches, projections, gates, and towers, not unlike a miniature city. Symmetry has replaced the earlier building's asymmetry, but with its small windows the addition appears, like the original building, hermetic. The earlier building's cubism has been clarified into a single, pure cube, and the rough materiality of that 1958 building has been simplified to a gleaming skin, albeit one with visual depth, being of basalt. Like most of Ungers' work over the past twenty-five years, the addition's forms are based largely on the square and the cube; the basic form, of course, is a cube. The plan consists of squares within squares, square skylights pop out from the roof, and small, square windows dot the facades.

The peristyle court (above), filled with free-standing Doric columns, is a metaphor for the public square as well as the cloister. To one side of the court is the asymmetrical older building, and to another is the pure cube of the library (left).

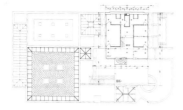

ROOF

FIRST FLOOR

GROUND FLOOR

The theme of a house within a house, as in Ungers' German Architecture Museum of the early 1980s, is explored here, with the ground floor of the two-story cube surrounded by a skylit one-story structure. The cube is lined with books (which will become, after Ungers' death, the Ungers Archive for Architectural Science), and in the center is a white cubic skeleton, the "basic element of architecture." This overlay of forms produces spatial complexity, a variety of natural light sources, and a juxtaposition of smooth materials against more tactile ones (some from the older building) and light-colored structural members against dark-painted fittings. In the layering of spaces and surprising light effects, the Cube House is reminiscent, in a more rationalized way, of the John Soane House in London, which was also built to house one architect's private but museum-worthy collection. ∎

In a room lit by four square skylights (above and facing page), dark-lacquered bookshelves line the walls and surround a white cubic frame symbolizing the "essence" of architecture.

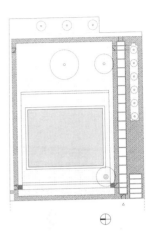

If the Cube House of 1989 (page 102) represented a way station on the architectural voyage of O. M. Ungers' career, the Ungers House III represents an end point. In his journey, he has moved from the rough materiality and asymmetry of his early works through the rationalism and symmetrical abstraction of his middle and later works, and has arrived at a work of absolute purity, in which nothing distracts from the perfect calm of the finely proportioned Platonic form. The Ungers House III reaches a level of flawlessness comparable to Mies van der Rohe's 1946 Farnsworth House. However, where the latter never limits the visual flow of space but demarcates planes within the universe, the Ungers House III is the ultimate container. There is the House, and then there is the rest of the world.

The two-story stuccoed building, 39 by 52 by 26 feet high (proportionally 3:4:2), stands on a stone plinth within an enclosed garden in a residential neighborhood in Cologne. Ungers has designed the house as a pure art object within a garden of paradise. The garden itself is bordered by a hedge of yews, kept trimmed to a height of 10 feet. The purity of the relationship between the natural space and the art object is "disturbed" only by the random location of existing trees (or "tree objects," as the architect puts it) on the site.

The pure white house stands within a garden enclosed by hedges (left).
The garden is entered from the street through a yew-lined pergola (above).

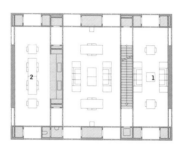

GROUND FLOOR

1 LIVING ROOM
2 DINING ROOM
3 BEDROOM

One enters the site through a pergola that runs along its southern edge. From here, the first spatial layer, the green space, is penetrated and crossed, and then the plinth is mounted. There is no single main entrance into the house; all doors are equal: the usual entry hierarchy is abandoned in order to achieve abstraction.

The house has only five rooms. On the ground floor are the central two-story space, which the architect refers to as the *salla terrena*, and two 12-foot-wide by 12-foot-high side naves, one serving as kitchen and dining room, the other as living room. On the second story, the side naves hold the private quarters (the *studioli*) of Ungers and his wife. The underground level holds a pristine swimming pool. Materials are natural but understated: stuccolustro plaster for the walls, and floors of limestone in the *salla terrena*, terra cotta in the ground-floor side naves, and wood in the upper-floor side naves.

Running along the east and west edges of the house and between the side naves and the central space are 5-foot-thick zones that contain the stairs, closets, and other storage rooms, cabinets, and the bathrooms. Ungers designed these edge zones following the principles of Roman walls; they have carefully finished outer and inner shells encasing prosaic contents.

The central two-story salla terrena *(above) is flanked by side rooms, one of them the kitchen/dining room (facing page). Both rooms are furnished with tables and chairs designed by the architect.*

Architectural historian Francesco Dal Co, in an essay about this residence, compares it to the house designed in 1926 by the philosopher Ludwig Wittgenstein for his sister. In its austerity and its exacting attention to measurements and proportions, this comparison is apt. As if following Wittgenstein's dictum in his *Tractatus*, what Ungers could say, he said clearly; the unsayable he left unsaid. Dal Co also likens aspects of the Ungers House III to the pure, unadulterated spaces of the early modern architect Adolf Loos. But Dal Co concludes that this house—in its desperate search for spiritual unity, its attempts to reconcile opposites, and its efforts to make order of our complex existences—represents most of all a grappling with the ideas of early-nineteenth-century German architect Karl Friedrich Schinkel.

Ungers himself explains that the house represents a fundamental architectural typology, based on the three-bayed floor plan with central bay and two side naves, a type that has appeared in countless stylistic variations through the ages. Ungers' own variation is characterized by the rejection of all superfluous elements. He makes no reference to historical details. There are in this design, says Ungers, no synonyms for anything, no layers of meaning, just the unadulterated core.

As the architect summarizes, "At the end of a long and eventful history, a history laden with content and full of symbols and metaphors, stands the geometrically purified box." ∎

The pristine nature of the underground pool (above) is in keeping with the abstract perfection of the white volume of the house (facing and following pages). Finished in encausto stucco, the house stands on a base of Vermont limestone.

BARONE POTTGIESSER, ARCHITECTS
PARIS

HOUSE/**BARN** CHARGEY-LÈS-PORT, FRANCE

Several years ago, Christian Pottgiesser and his two brothers bought a large seventeenth-century mill structure in the Haute-Sâone region of France to serve as a communal vacation home. The family "camped out" in the huge tentlike shelter until some members felt the need for more creature comforts. That is when the German-born, French-educated Pottgiesser and his wife and colleague, Sonia Barone, took action to restore and adapt the venerable edifice.

Pottgiesser and Barone divided the square plan into three parallel zones. The zone along one side was maintained as barn space, and the zone along the other side was converted to two stories of living spaces—three bedroom suites and a kitchen/sitting area. These two zones retain the original architectural character, with features that are largely preexisting—big, rough-hewn wood columns and beams, partially stuccoed stone walls, and oak windows and doors. The central zone, however, now contains a totally unique insertion. While the original soaring space continues to be completely visible, a long concrete structure has been added. The new two-story structure, 4 feet wide and 40 feet long, incorporates stairs, bathrooms, and a quiet "retreat" alcove.

A modern concrete structure (facing page) was inserted into a two-hundred-year-old stone mill building (above), now a vacation home for three brothers and their families.

The entire structure is calibrated to serve as a sundial. A large skylight over the entrance door (facing page) allows light to enter the building and fall upon markings on the walls and floor (above). A small metal square in the center of the skylight casts a shadow on the exact time designation.

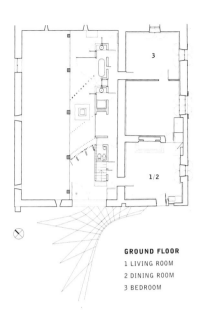

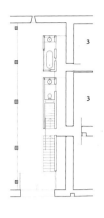

GROUND FLOOR
1 LIVING ROOM
2 DINING ROOM
3 BEDROOM

UPPER FLOOR
RENOVATIONS ONLY

Architectural observers will note a similarity to the late work of Le Corbusier in the new concrete structure, whose finish reflects its wood formwork and whose hieroglyphic-like drawings are reminiscent of the modern master's illustrative figures. Moreover, the sunlight that gleams through the small high windows in the perimeter walls and roof recalls the radiance of Le Corbusier's nearby chapel at Ronchamp. In the manner in which the concrete structure integrates inventive features, such as interestingly detailed wood stairs and oddly proportioned wood-framed rectangular windows, the design is suggestive as well of the work of the twentieth-century Italian architect Carlo Scarpa.

Pottgiesser does claim to be an admirer of Le Corbusier and Scarpa. But his major inspiration for this structure was the concept of an architecturally framed sundial. He installed a skylight in the roof, with a 6-inch-square metal plate at its center, so that a small shadow surrounded by an illuminated square enables time to be read with accuracy. To calibrate the building to serve as a sundial, the architect carefully positioned a series of markings throughout the central zone. Oak figures were inset into the floor, hieroglyphic incisions were made in the concrete walls, and even the holes made by the formwork bolts were specially located.

A philosopher as well as an architect, Pottgiesser explains that the building-as-sundial allows humans to balance conflicting sensations about our place in the universe: unnerving thoughts about openness and relativity, and consoling thoughts about our control of the environment. Among the contrivances we devise to achieve such control are sundials, which allow us to measure the relationship between two heavenly bodies, and buildings, which we erect to reassure ourselves of our place on earth. Therefore, concludes Pottgiesser, chronomorphic structures tie us to the cosmos in a way that is simultaneously comforting and liberating. ∎

The new structure (facing page) incorporates stairs leading to the second-story bedrooms and attic (above), where elements of the original barn structure were preserved.

122

From the large bathtubs on both levels of the new structure
(above and right), residents can relax and, through
low corner windows, watch the evidence of time passing.

HERZOG & DE MEURON ARCHITECTS
BASEL, SWITZERLAND

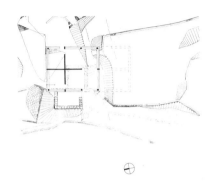

Swiss architects Jacques Herzog and Pierre de Meuron are known for work that is both intensely cerebral and sensuous. Among the projects for which they are recognized internationally are the conversion of the Bankside Power Station in London into the Tate Gallery of Modern Art, completed in 1999, and their highly acclaimed (though unselected) competition entry for a major addition to the Museum of Modern Art in New York. The romantic-cum-intellectual nature of their work is evident in, among other projects, the rigorous stone Dominus Winery in California's Napa Valley, their only large built project in the United States, as well as the Stone House in Tavole, shown here.

The three-story house in the Ligurian mountains emerges almost naturalistically from an undulating landscape of abandoned olive groves. Standing on a promontory, it engages part of a former stone terrace, which in turn forms a continuum with the low walls that meander through the surrounding countryside. The walls of the house consist of rubblelike stone set without mortar. Such masonry walls are still commonly built in the area, and they connect visually to both the rocky landscape and traditional local architecture.

A grid of concrete, which extends beyond the building, frames stone walls (facing page) similar to those typically found in this mountainous region of northwest Italy (above).

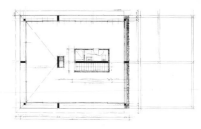

UPPER FLOOR

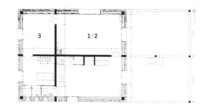

FIRST FLOOR
1 LIVING ROOM
2 DINING ROOM
3 BEDROOM

The house's reinforced-concrete structure constitutes the rational component of the design. Within the 2,000-square-foot house, two perpendicular concrete walls intersect to create a cross in plan. This cruciform theme is expressed on the exterior walls by a concrete skeleton—the extrapolation of the interior walls and the floor and roof slabs—that forms the framework for the stone infill. The concrete skeleton is extended beyond the house in the form of a gridded pergola defining the raised terrace.

In a published interview the architects draw an analogy between this design and the form of a mountain, whose basic structure is determined by its mineral formation, linking it, say, to limestone mountains everywhere, while its external layer bears the imprint of the local weather and vegetation. Thus, the three-dimensional concrete grid represents for the architects the idea of "serial" design, since, like a crystalline structure, it can theoretically be repeated infinitely. Abstract and unlimited, it has no site-specific significance. In contrast, explain the architects, the stone infill roots the house to its site.

Similarly, the cruciform plan of the concrete walls conveys a worldly, abstract image, while the disposition of these interior walls on the main floor of the house reveal a peasant tradition. The partitions simply define four rooms (bedrooms, kitchen, and bathroom) without corridors, so that servant and served functions are united. On the top floor, some of the internal walls are dissolved to form one large studio space. In this space, strip windows provide panoramic views of the countryside.

The detailing of the house is spare: window shutters consist of steel sheets, and door and window linings are of split slate pieces. These details, like the concrete walls, reveal once again the congruence of modern and primitive design. ∎

Stone retaining walls, like those meandering through the landscape, form a terrace off the first floor (facing page). The main living floor is fenestrated almost traditionally (above) while the top floor, which serves as an open studio, offers spectacular views through strip windows on three sides. The concrete grid (following pages) extends to demarcate the terrace.

KLAUS KADA, ARCHITECT
GRAZ, AUSTRIA

HOUSE **KADA B.** LEIBNITZ, AUSTRIA

The provincial town of Graz has been home over the last three decades to a school of architecture whose proponents are united mainly by creative energy and antiestablishment fervor. These Graz architects have consistently distinguished themselves from "academic" architects. They distanced themselves, first of all, from Vienna, which they view as the repository of the establishment and the mainstay of academicism. In the early 1980s, they reacted against Miesian modernism, to produce an ebullient expressionistic outpouring replete with voluptuously sculptural and even anthropomorphic forms. In the late 1980s and '90s, they rebelled against classical postmodernism, switching gears and returning to the use of straight lines and large planes of glass—not that far from Mies, after all, nor from Vienna's conspicuous bad-boy firm, Coop Himmelblau.

Klaus Kada emerged in the late 1980s as a prominent member of the Graz avant-garde, with work that is cool and well ordered and betrays a special veneration for glass. Glass, he says, permits technological freedom (he contrasts the laborious laying of stone upon stone with the installation of a modern sheet of glass) and psychological liberation (he feels that the material implies openness, freedom, ease of communication—in short, democratic principles).

A mahogany-stained plywood "box" is added alongside a small, hundred-year-old house (right). The two parts are linked by a two-story all-glass stair hall.

While the plywood "box" seems solid when viewed from the street, folding doors in its side wall and a back wall of louvers reveal that the rear of the box is, in fact, open (above).

Kada's cool discipline and, in a limited but crucial form, his special way with glass are apparent in the striking addition to the late-nineteenth-century house shown here, an addition that doubles the available space to about 4,000 square feet. A long, steel-framed, plywood-clad box is placed beside the existing house, its insistent, scaleless boxiness directly confronting the bourgeois, even kitsch, nature of the hundred-year-old residence. The original house was painstakingly preserved and its plaster facade was painted a saturated greenish-blue, the exact color complement to the strong reddish-brown chosen for the stain of the new wood box.

UPPER FLOOR

GROUND FLOOR
1 LIVING ROOM
2 DINING ROOM
3 BEDROOM

Three views of the central connecting pavilion show its glazed roof and parts of the old tiled roof within it.

To link the modern rectangular volume and the ornate original form, Kada used an all-glass connector—even the roof is glazed—as mediator. The decoratively articulated old house, with its somewhat complex roofs, is in part engulfed by the glass structure, but its integrity is never compromised. Even where part of the old roof is subsumed under the new glass roof, its details, including its gutter, are left intact. Not even a change in color marks the point where the old facade passes from an exterior to an interior condition.

As to the rectangular box, close inspection reveals that it is not as taut and closed a form as it seems to be. Two-thirds of its apparent volume encloses interior rooms: an entrance vestibule, powder room, and kitchen on the ground floor, and a study and bathroom above. The box's rear third, however, has only a side and an end wall, which serve as windscreen to the house's terrace. The end wall of the box is formed of wood louvers, and folding wood doors in the long side wall reveal that here, "inside" is actually "outside." As stern as it is compared to the fanciful older structure, this tightly drawn box most certainly plays games as well. ∎

The partially open rear of the plywood box screens the new deck (facing page). The deck is accessible from the kitchen, which is incorporated into the addition (above).

GASPAR HOUSE
CADIZ, SPAIN

In his description of the Gaspar House, Spanish architect Alberto Campo Baeza includes a medieval drawing of the Garden of Eden. Paradise is depicted as a perfect square, its orderly grove of trees separated from the surrounding chaos by a high wall. The white outer walls of the Gaspar House serve a similar function, excluding the noisy world outside from a more perfect inner sanctuary.

Campo Baeza terms his own work "essential architecture," by which he means architecture that has been not so much simplified as distilled. He prefers the word essential to the art-historical term minimalist and modifies Mies van der Rohe's motto "less is more" to "more with less." Whether essential or minimal, the Gaspar House underlines this willingness to eliminate all that is not strictly necessary, to pare down a design until it is impossible to imagine subtracting—or adding—anything at all.

A square within a square, the central volume of the Gaspar House rises above its enclosure (above). The inner courtyard, which lends iconic importance to the elements of everyday life (facing page) is a space of serene, austere beauty (following pages).

1 LIVING ROOM
2 DINING ROOM
3 BEDROOM

As defined and elucidated in the Gaspar House, the principle elements of architecture are geometry and light or, as phrased by Le Corbusier, whose influence on Campo Baeza is self-evident, "the masterly, correct, and magnificent play of masses brought together in light." The house's 12-foot outer walls describe a 60-by-60-foot square, which is divided into three equal and parallel parts: patio, house, and patio. The central pavilion rises 15 feet in height and is flanked to the north and south by two 12-foot-high service spaces containing bedrooms and a kitchen. Perpendicular to the axis formed by these three elements, two 6.5-foot walls running east to west cut through the patios and pavilion, creating a nine-unit grid of unequal parts. Four green lemon trees planted in the patios reinforce the double symmetry of the plan.

Fenestration is purposely limited to four square windows set at the point of intersection of the lower walls and the central pavilion. These large, simple openings provide, says Campo Baeza, a kind of horizontal light. Through them, inside and outside merge, with only light to decorate the whitewashed, weight-bearing masonry.

One reviewer has pointed out typological connections between the Gaspar House and the prototypical Roman house. At the same time, this archetypal architecture is also very economical. Built for a schoolteacher, the 1,200-square-foot Gaspar House cost only $70,000; it states an effective case for affordable high design, something Campo Baeza strongly advocates. ∎

The house's four windows are placed at the point of intersection of walls that create a nine-unit grid in plan (above). In the courtyard, a lime tree, a rectangular reflecting pool, and a pile of stones shape a composition of earth, water, and sky (facing page).

MARIO BOTTA ARCHITECT
LUGANO, SWITZERLAND

The elemental nature of primitive architecture has inspired modern architects for much of this century. Generally, the interpretation of primitive forms in modern architecture has produced "universal" forms based on pure geometries. In the rugged Ticino region of southern Switzerland, where centuries of poverty-driven pragmatism have produced an indigenous architecture of spare, rigorous forms, modern transformations by Ticinese regionalist architects, as they are called, have been less "complete." Agrarian forms remain recognizable, and the sense of rough-textured local materials has been re-created rather than suppressed in the modernist quest for abstraction. At the same time, the Ticinese architects have sought to create ideal geometries rather than functionally determined organic volumes, in keeping with the rationalist movements in Italy, led by Giuseppe Terragni in the 1930s and the *Tendenza* architects of the 1970s.

145

Among the architects currently identified with the Ticinese regionalist movement, Mario Botta is the best known internationally, both for his extensive domestic work and his imposing institutional buildings. The latter include the bold, fortresslike San Francisco Museum of Modern Art completed in 1994. An examination of Botta's architecture, especially his earliest work, reveals the influence of Louis Kahn and Le Corbusier, with whom Botta worked early in his career.

The tall symmetrical house (facing page), which is built into the mountain, is punctuated with glass-roofed terraces that offer panoramic views of the surrounding hills (above).

With the success of his growing practice, Botta has remained faithful to his instinct for sturdy forms and his interest in ideal geometries, but many of his recent houses are elaborate in shape. The 2,300-square-foot house at Daro is a case in point. Its wedge-shaped plan and symmetrical facade, while strong, are complex rather than elemental. The lightweight metal frame of its roof has an ornamental quality, more delicate than the elements of his earlier houses. As always, Botta manages to balance lightness and mass: the arched glass roof contrasts poignantly with the mass of the masonry as well as with the solemn rectilinear openings carved deep into its volume. As is typical in Botta's buildings, the masonry is beautifully detailed and creates an integral pattern of horizontal stripes: in the main facade of the Daro house, rows of flat cement blocks alternate with similar blocks laid at 45-degree angles.

The skylit stairway (above), which has at its center a sculptural metal handrail, runs up the back corner of the four-story house. On the top two floors, the library/music room overlooks the living/dining room, both of which lead to terraces with spectacular views (right).

THIRD FLOOR

SECOND FLOOR

1

2

FIRST FLOOR

1 LIVING ROOM
2 DINING ROOM
3 BEDROOM

3

3

GROUND FLOOR

In its relationship to its surroundings, the Daro House combines two themes frequently found in Botta's work. The house, half buried in the hillside, is both cave and belvedere, a traditional building type in the mountainous Ticinese landscape. Except at the topmost floor of this four-story house, the rooms are introverted, so that the sense of protection is manifest. But each room has a terrace, and the terraces focus on the dramatic views into the valley. The passage through the house leads from darkness to full light—from the earth to the sky. Entering through the lowest level, an underground zone largely occupied by utility rooms, one is drawn to the skylit staircase at the back of the house. The view is revealed only gradually as one ascends through the house. In the half-buried bedroom story, each room has a corner window recessed behind small balconies. In the main living area on the next floor, spaces are arranged as a U around a central loggia, so that the outlook from the central space is narrowed and views from each side space are oblique. At the top, one emerges at the library/music room, where at last the windows reveal a panoramic vista. In this room and on the adjacent glass-roofed terraces, one feels liberated by the sky and the boundless views. ∎

The house's sturdy form is enlivened by the texture of its materials: a delicate metal-framed glass roof and walls of gray cement blocks (facing page). The blocks are laid up flat or angled on each alternate row.

JOHN YOUNG, ARCHITECT
LONDON

THE **DECK HOUSE** LONDON

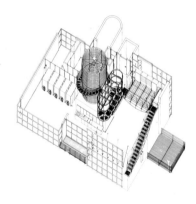

Twenty-two years after its first major monument, the Pompidou Center, opened its doors in Paris, the high-tech movement is still going strong, especially in England. The remarkable staying power of this particular branch of twentieth-century modernism is unique to that country, where it unites architects whose work can be quite diverse in detail. In their hands, the traditional academic emphasis on space-making and formal composition takes a back seat to the celebration of architectural construction: how a building is made determines what it looks like.

As a member of the international team that designed the Pompidou Center, architect John Young was there at the beginning of high tech, and he is there still, both as a partner in the Richard Rogers Partnership and as the architect for his own penthouse apartment atop a housing block on the Thames River designed by the Rogers office. The 3,000-square-foot apartment, a tour de force in high-tech design, celebrates the machinery in the "machine for living," as Le Corbusier described the modern house. Every element in this rooftop world has been rethought, from the curved glass doors that hide the lavatory and the laundry to the "wind beam," a bow truss bracing the double-height window-wall in the living room. Many details, such as landing lights inset into the concrete floor, are crossover elements scouted from other fields. Believing that the maritime and aeronautical industries meet higher standards than the traditional building industry, Young went to them and other sources still farther afield for custom manufacture. The decks of the apartment, like those in boats, are laid in teak, and the floodlights are adopted from Italian photography studio equipment. Wall-mounted platecoil heaters, which boost the underfloor heating, come from a Texas manufacturer of massive heat ranges for industrial applications. Even the stainless steel bidet is adapted from a vandal-proof toilet designed for public lavatories.

A world apart from its Hammersmith neighbors (above), this penthouse apartment enjoys spectacular views of the Thames River. Floor-to-ceiling glazing is strengthened by a specially designed bow truss. Circular wall-hung heating units utilize technology developed for the chemical industry (facing page).

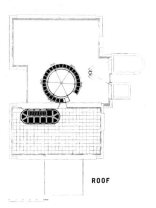

ROOF

MEZZANINE LEVEL

ENTRY LEVEL
1 LIVING ROOM
2 DINING ROOM
3 BEDROOM

153

*The stair of graduated risers leads up to the sleeping loft.
The only element of the apartment not designed by Young
is the furniture, some of which is by Le Corbusier.*

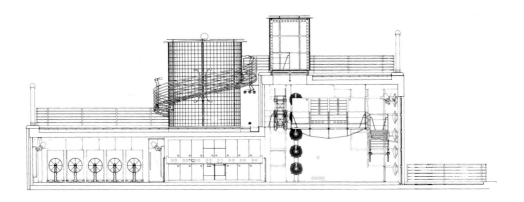

If there is any overarching metaphor behind this design, it is that of ships and the lighthouses that guide them. A glazed observatory on the uppermost terrace surfaces above the apartment block like a crow's nest. The circular master bath glows at night like the lamp chamber of a lighthouse, its gridded glass facade cut by the curved line of an encircling ramp. The river itself and its changeable weather are freely admitted, at least visually, into the main living space through floor-to-ceiling glazing, and are reflected in stainless steel finishes or waxed concrete floors. There is admittedly little here that caters to traditional domestic comfort. Clutter is hidden in huge mobile storage units, whose movement on tracks in the floor is controlled by yachting wheels. The master bedroom is not a room at all but a loft suspended above the living room by four slender stainless steel rods. More conventional bedrooms for Young's grown children and guests occupy a self-contained flat to the rear of the apartment that can be accessed separately from the entrance lobby.

The motivation behind the design of these details is not utilitarian—this is not an architecture that seeks the simplest or easiest solution to a problem. The apartment is instead a kind of proving ground in which a whole century of technological development is celebrated and tested. It is no surprise that Young should consider the French architects Jean Prouvé and Pierre Chareau his heroes, for they too pushed the construction materials and methods of their day to the limit, creating a density of detail that is its own aesthetic. The bath tower is itself a kind of homage to Chareau, recalling his seminal Maison de Verre of 1932.

In the apartment, only the furniture is not of Young's design. Instead, the architect chose classic examples of high modern design: Le Corbusier's armchair, for example, and a mirror by Eileen Gray. He explains simply that he is not interested in designing furniture, turning his eye instead to the turnbolts of a stair tread. There is in this tinkering a hidden optimism, a quiet faith in the power of invention to make something truly new and beautiful. ∎

Elements such as the steel trusses supporting the stair and loft (above) are painted in the signature primary colors associated with the work of the Richard Rogers office, where Young is a partner.

*Metal kitchen cabinets are finished in a moiré pattern copied from delivery trucks in Tokyo (facing page),
while the wheels that control the motion of massive storage cabinets are typically used for yachts (above).
On the upper floor, the sleeping loft is connected to the master bathroom by a catwalk (following pages).*

The cylindrical glass-block master bathroom (facing page and above) recalls the Maison de Verre of Pierre Chareau. The room is encircled by a ramp leading to the upper terrace and observatory.

ARCHITECTURE STUDIO
PARIS

HOUSE ON RUE ROBERT BLACHE PARIS

What does it mean to be modern in Paris, a city whose image is so strongly rooted in the nineteenth century, a city in which architecture has always been a political act, not only in the era of Baron Haussmann, its principal designer, but now? Founded in Paris in the early 1970s as a collaborative practice dedicated to the social and political art of architecture, Architecture Studio is no stranger to the city or its politics. Working in collaboration with Jean Nouvel and others, the firm won the competition to design the Institut du Monde Arabe in the early 1980s, ushering in the era of the so-called *grands projets*, through which French President François Mitterrand promised to change the face of Paris. Most recently, Architecture Studio completed the commission to design the European Parliament building in Strasbourg, a project that symbolizes a new political order in Europe. The house on Rue Robert Blache is therefore the relatively private exception to a very public practice whose portfolio is more likely to contain public high schools, old-age homes, and university buildings than single-family houses.

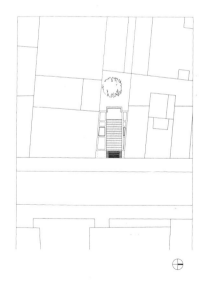

The street façade respects the height and frontage of its nondescript neighbors. The white walls that define this modern insertion are curved at the top to recall the profile of a typical nineteenth-century Parisian townhouse.

The stair's metal cage is reminiscent of those used to enclose stairs or elevators in countless European townhouses and apartment buildings (above and facing page, bottom). Rooms on the front of the house are lit by horizontal windows (facing page, top).

In its simple plan and section, the 2,000-square-foot townhouse summarizes the universal concerns of urban dwellings everywhere, but especially in Paris: the relationship of building to street and the maximization of natural light. The design defines the edges of its tiny, 30-by-16-foot site through the use of two buffer zones delineated in concrete. These thick walls, which also serve to set the house apart from its unremarkable neighbors, are curved at the top to echo the profile of traditional Parisian garrets. The volume between defines a pure rectangle 30 by 10 feet in plan that is set perpendicular to the street, in order, say the architects, to reestablish the orthogonal city grid. Its facade, clad in smooth mahogany, is tilted toward the sun.

Sunlight is in fact the principal object of the house's interior organization. The house section reveals a greater complexity than its plan would suggest. At the heart of the house, a steel staircase rises in a metal cage, whose open grid allows a maximum of light to penetrate as deeply into the townhouse as possible. The rear rooms are staggered a half floor below the front rooms, again to maximize daylight penetration. The interior is treated as one vertical space; where privacy is necessary or desirable, curtains can be closed over glass walls separating bedrooms from the central stair.

This almost relentless transparency, coupled with the staggering of half floors, has the effect of transforming the townhouse prototype. The traditional townhouse is conceived as a stacking of floors running straight through from street to rear yard, its darkest section at the heart of the building. By contrast, the townhouse on Rue Robert Blache is organized vertically, not horizontally, around a stair that doubles as light well. The architectural solution, in its resolution of a very old urban problem, is as sensible as it is aesthetically satisfying. ■

FOURTH FLOOR

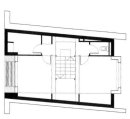

THIRD FLOOR

SECOND FLOOR

FIRST FLOOR

Light is the main decorative element, with ribbon windows casting a variety of patterns on white interior walls (facing page and above).

DRIENDL*STEIXNER, ARCHITECTS
VIENNA

STANDARD SOLAR HOUSE LANGENSCHÖNBICHL, AUSTRIA

Le Corbusier began the modernist process of "clearing up" architecture many decades ago, note architects Georg Driendl and Gerhard Steixner. But even now the technology for house-building remains in the dark ages, they point out, compared to the progress that has been made, for example, in the design and performance of home entertainment equipment.

For this reason, the two of them designed this house—the first full-scale prototype of the prefabricated, solar-heated building system they devised—as a manifesto. Through it, they wished to prove the efficacy of starting from "inside" a problem: that is, from what is needed, and not from traditional notions of what a house should look like. They use all-glass walls, for example, not primarily for aesthetic reasons but because they admit more sun and are simpler to build than framed glass windows within traditional walls. They specify wood for the floor-to-ceiling operable panels also as a matter of economy. The architects admit, however, that they relish the irony implicit in switching the roles of opaque and transparent materials, with glass *not* used for operable windows, and opaque "walls" *not* being fixed.

On the front facade of the house, fixed sheets of glass alternate with solid doors of wood and cork (above). Solar energy enters the house through this south-facing glass wall and through a sloped glass roof (top). Translucent polycarbonate panels can slide across the glass wall (facing page) to keep heat in during cold weather.

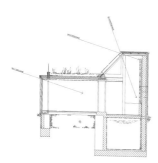

In their attempt to make progress in the design and performance of houses, the architects seem to have succeeded with this standard solar prototype. The house, they report, was 20 percent cheaper to build than a traditional house of its size and, now inhabited by a family of five, costs 40 percent less to heat. Furthermore, with its long, elegantly glazed front, its discreetly lush materials, its rhythmic modularity, its small reflecting ponds, and its open interior spaces, it looks nothing like the earnest, whole-earth image typical of its genre.

The impact of the architects' experiment, however, has been less widespread than anticipated. Acceptance of the product (the kit of parts and design) has been slow. Though it is marketed for use as house, professional office, or work studio and can be adapted to enclose between 1,300 and 2,000 square feet of space, only two additional houses have been built in the decade since the first 1,800-square-foot one was completed.

Except for the massive concrete wall on its north side, the house is built of a light standardized structure of glue-laminated wood beams and wood and tubular steel columns. Walls are made of standardized panels of glass or cork sandwiched between wood. The house consists of three zones: the large south-facing rectangular main living area, divisible into two bedrooms and a living room; a tall, long and narrow greenhouse/bathroom on the north side behind the main living space; and the two-story east pavilion, containing an eat-in kitchen on the ground floor and the master bedroom above.

The standardized structural system offers numerous layout possibilities, as can be seen in this view (right) taken before interior partitions were installed. In the rear is the bathroom, the thick stone wall of which (above) stores solar energy penetrating the glass roof.

The south-facing wing employs passive energy strategies. On sunny winter days, the large sheets of insulated glass in its main facade allow rays of sun (including those reflected from pools beside the house) to penetrate this zone and heat it. On hot summer days, aluminum louvers on the exterior can shade the glass, while at night and on very cold days, interior sliding panels of translucent polycarbonate can be drawn across the wall to minimize heat loss. The roof over this south-facing zone is covered in turf to help moderate heat loss and gain, a feature that, furthermore, provides a lawn accessible from the second level.

The northern zone, which is one and a half stories high, employs an active strategy. As sunlight enters its high, sloped, south-facing glass roof (shaded during the summer by canvas), the rays hit the basalt stone finish—400 square feet in all—of the 2-foot-thick, insulated reinforced concrete north wall. The heat is collected in water-filled pipes behind the basalt, and the warmed water is transferred to a 2,000-cubic-foot storage chamber in the ground and circulated to warm the spaces through convection heaters and, in the kitchen and greenhouse/bathroom, through pipes under the stone floor. A gas-driven heat exchange system provides supplemental heat if necessary during extreme winter weather.

Over the kitchen (above), a second-story space can be used as the master bedroom (facing page).

LOWER FLOOR

1 LIVING ROOM
2 DINING ROOM
3 BEDROOM

UPPER FLOOR

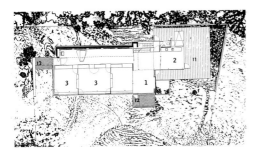

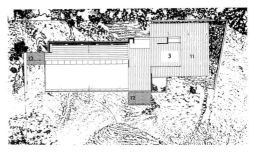

With each practical move, the architects have reaped an aesthetic benefit as well. The different ceiling heights essential for the solar strategies in the north and south zones create exceptional spatial drama. The varied finishes needed for insulation and absorption have resulted in a rich palette of materials: basalt wall, marble flooring, poplar and beech wall panels, shoji-like translucent screens. And the extensive glazing required for heat collection has led to an especially close bond between interior spaces and the landscape. In this eloquent case of "form following function," both parts of the equation achieve a very high performance level indeed. ∎

174

A number of the wall sections of the kitchen can be folded open, to create an almost open room during the summer.

EDUARDO SOUTO DE MOURA ARCHITECTS
PORTO, PORTUGAL

BOM JESUS HOUSE
BRAGA, PORTUGAL

Eduardo Souto de Moura belongs to the post-Siza generation of architects in Portugal, those who matured in the long but somehow comfortable shadow of their nation's most famous modernist. Souto de Moura, who worked for Alvaro Siza, believes in the power of architecture to serve as a source of equilibrium and stability in society—not an expression of late-twentieth-century chaos but its antidote.

The Bom Jesus House, for example, is both universal and particular. In it, Souto de Moura seeks to reconcile the "mass-produced-for-everyman" aspect of modern design with place-specific traditions of construction and craftsmanship that have prevailed in Portugal for centuries. The house is at once severe yet sensual, minimalist yet richly textured. It is on the one hand a composition of abstract forms—a blue, rectangular pool set perpendicular to a white, rectangular wall, for example—and on the other, a rich mix of present and past, of I-beams and hand-cut stones.

177

The house is a blend of classically modern principles and local building technology. The entrance stair leads to the upper-level living spaces and a terrace that runs behind the stone wall (left and following pages).

Set into the top of a hillside overlooking the city of Braga, the house's long granite wall runs across the high terrain like the outer reach of a medieval castle. Behind this rough stone embankment rises a glass pavilion outlined in crisp white lines. At the western end, the 4,800-square-foot house seems to slip past its protective outer wall, presenting a grand outdoor stair adjacent to the actual entrance hall that leads up to a south-facing terrace along which the main living spaces are strung. This upper floor plan is almost archetypally modern in its organization. Service elements—kitchen, baths, and corridors—form a second, long zone along the back of the house, opening to a terrace of grass, which is allowed to run like a smooth carpet all the way up to the rear glass facade.

180

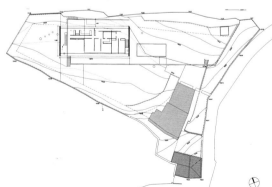

Both machined and handcrafted techniques are visible in the entrance hall (above), where a metal stair rises against a traditional stone wall. The interior is spacious (facing page, top), with a limited palette of materials that have been carefully detailed (facing page, bottom).

The shallower ground floor, cut into the hillside, is occupied by a garage and a children's living room, guest room and bath, the latter spaces lit by simple rectangular openings cut through the stone wall and glazed. These barnlike openings are simply framed with lintels and stones of varying sizes; from certain angles, moreover, the single sheets of glass, which are free of any distracting mullions, seem to disappear into shadow.

Although this stone wall may recall the traditional, vernacular architecture of the region, the reference is neither picturesque nor romantic. Instead, traditional techniques are used here in the service of a very modern sensibility. Nowhere is this more evident than in the entrance hall, where a lightweight stair of thin wooden treads and pipe rail supported on an industrial I-beam rises against a rough-cut stone wall set with pebble mortar. In his attempts to shape a regional modernism, Souto de Moura has succeeded in wedding the light, open possibilities of modern construction to the strong, protective associations of vernacular architecture. ▪

LOWER FLOOR

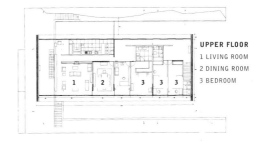

UPPER FLOOR
1 LIVING ROOM
2 DINING ROOM
3 BEDROOM

The house nestles into the hillside near its crown (facing page and top, above). The pool area is a more purely abstract composition (above).

CHRISTOPH MÄCKLER ARCHITECTS
FRANKFURT-ON-MAIN, GERMANY

HOUSE **ADDITION** CONSTANCE, GERMANY

The narrow end of the 12-by-60-foot addition is visible from Lake Constance, so that the three-hundred-year-old winery building remains the prominent structure (above and facing page).

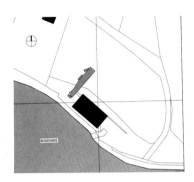

Christoph Mäckler feels strongly about what he terms the "rematerialization" of the modern, and he has been outspoken, in writing and in public, about his thesis. Most thoughtful architects would concur with these beliefs, which include an advocacy of responsible, ecologically sensitive planning and a rejection of skin-deep form-giving. In support of these beliefs, Mäckler calls for a true understanding on the part of architects of how materials and current technologies function. He also calls for a deeper understanding of architectural history, including the now varied and rich history of modern architecture.

A most happy outcome of Mäckler's own understanding of both materials and modern history is seen on these pages, a 2,000-square-foot residential addition to a stone winery structure on the shores of Lake Constance. The family who dwelled in the upper story of the sixteenth-century structure (the ground level is too damp for habitation) had, with the advent of a fifth child, outgrown the accommodations. Since the building is listed as a historic structure, the owners turned to Mäckler to expand their living space while respecting the legislated design limitations.

Following his own well-publicized principles, Mäckler began with careful and respectful planning. He designed the new building as a thin slip of a structure, 12 feet wide along the lakefront and 60 feet deep, allowing the wide existing structure its primacy in the view from the lake. This gave him the leeway to make the new building quite distinct in form and materials from the older building, underscoring the individuality of both structures.

The new long, thin building, which serves as a belvedere overlooking the lake, sits atop a square, half-buried room, also new. This bunkerlike room, with thick, implicitly protective double walls, serves as the communal space, and the belvedere wing holds the four individual bedrooms at either end of its long expanse. The square bunker is built, appropriately enough, of raw concrete, while the belvedere wing, ethereal in nature, is rendered in white stucco. The kitchen and bathroom—the service areas of the house—are each treated as protruding concrete boxes, one projecting from the square communal room, the other from the bedroom wing. The connection between new and existing buildings is made with an enclosed bridge of glass, considered by Mäckler one of the "noble" modern materials.

A glass bridge connects the new structure to the old (above). In the addition's south- and west-facing facades, brightly painted wood box frames with operable windows are inserted into fixed glass walls (above and facing page).

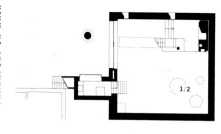

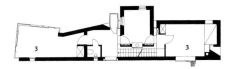

SECOND FLOOR

The raw concrete box housing the bathroom protrudes from the long, west-facing facade of the stuccoed addition (left). The addition is supported by a thick concrete column (above) as it projects beyond the half-buried living room, which is lit by skylights imbedded into playful forms on its roof (top, above).

There can be no doubt that the architect enjoyed himself enormously in making this building; one must look no further than the overall structure to be convinced. The long, thin wing, which extends beyond the bunker until it stands well above the sloping ground, is held up (or pinned down?) by a conical concrete pillar. Furthermore, where the long wing passes over the bunker, a space separates the two parts. Four ball-bearing supports hold the two elements apart; one can imagine the long wing spinning on its handle-like pillar, like a noisemaker at a New Year's Eve party.

The amusingly decorated shower room (facing page, top) is part of the enfilade of rooms, one leading to another, on the house's top floor (above). The bedrooms/study (facing page, bottom) facing the lake are opened up to the view by means of fully glazed walls on two sides.

Mäckler alludes to the early modern masters liberally. The conical concrete pillar and dematerialized white stucco form, its sides subtly bent and indented, are more than a little reminiscent of Le Corbusier, and the primary-colored window panels are suggestive of Gerrit Rietveld. Surely no one can overlook the exuberant high-tech positioning of the radiators in front of the glazed walls at the lakeside corner of the belvedere. And these glazed walls themselves are unusually detailed: operable windows in shadow boxes are inserted into fixed glass panes. Sail-like awnings shade these large glass expanses.

Does the house support Mäckler's thesis of "rematerialization?" Emphatically yes, at the micro if not the macro level, and the concept is executed in a refined yet jubilant manner that matches the fervor but not the sternness of Christoph Mäckler's words. ▪

The thin addition (right) sits on ball-bearings over the partially underground living room structure. The narrow kitchen (above) projects out from the living room.

ZUCCHI ARCHITECTS
MILAN

The single-family house, known in Italy as the *villetta*, has increasingly become part of the city's extended landscape. In the Padana flatland outside of Milan, where this house by Cino Zucchi is built, as in similar areas on the outskirts of other cities, residential development has been encroaching on territory formerly used for agrarian and industrial purposes. But on the typical suburban lot, the house is positioned in the center of the site as if it were truly a villa within a private park, and this arrangement uses the land inefficiently, notes Zucchi, who cites architects Serge Chermayeff and Christopher Alexander's critiques of English suburbs for confirmation.

In designing this private house, Zucchi—a professor at the Milan Polytechnic and the architect of numerous large-scale urban projects including, currently, a housing scheme in Venice—was determined to find a new solution for the suburban lot. Turning to Chermayeff and Alexander for help in redressing the perceived problems, he adapted ideas they promulgated during the 1960s for "courtgarden" designs in multiple housing. He applied aspects of the courtgarden house to the free-standing pavilionlike form typically found on suburban lots, a form mandated, in fact, by setback requirements, and came up with an unusual layout for this site.

The house's long mass is hollowed out to provide terraces at the second level (above and facing page). The roofed and partially enclosed courtyard serves as entrance court as well as outdoor living space, an arrangement that maximizes the use of the lot.

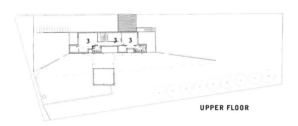

UPPER FLOOR

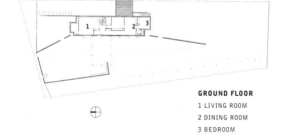

GROUND FLOOR
1 LIVING ROOM
2 DINING ROOM
3 BEDROOM

Following the example of the courtgarden house, Zucchi turned the house 90 degrees from its standard orientation on the site, putting its narrow end toward the street. He located the house in the northeast corner of the 85-by-240-foot site, as close to the front and side lot lines as the building code permitted, thereby combining the standard front garden and side lot in a large walled courtyard to the west, from which all access to the house occurs. The south end of the site, the end farthest from the street, was left in a natural state and planted with a grove of trees.

Zucchi designed the 1,800-square-foot house as a long, relatively narrow two-story structure running perpendicular to the street, so that the major rooms could be arranged alongside the courtyard. Rather than pandering to the typical suburban nostalgia for "traditional" forms, he designed a spare, brick-clad rectilinear volume modulated by large- and small-scale indentations. Cubes are hollowed out of the upper

The internal spaces, including the living room (facing page), are simply arranged along the length of the rectangular house. The minimally fenestrated east side of the house (above), like the adjacent driveway ramp, is located close to the side lot line and conveys an almost urban impression.

level to produce terraces for the bedrooms, and, on the west facade, bricks are laid in alternate projecting rows to create a banded appearance. The banding, says Zucchi, suggests a continuous form that can be elongated, as in the great brick industrial buildings of earlier times.

The house, while modern in appearance, functions like a traditional farmhouse with its generous courtyard and over-scaled portico that serves as a huge veranda. With the living and dining rooms leading directly out to the courtyard, family life moves easily between outside and in. ▪

198

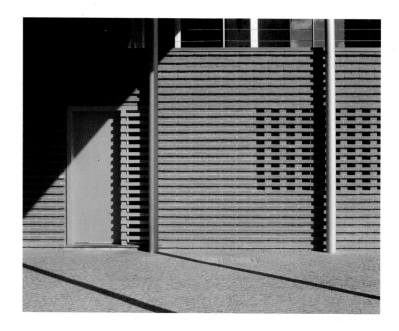

The west facade is modulated by bands of projecting brick (above and facing page). Open brickwork, as well as shadows cast by the portico's columns, further enliven the wall. The portico roof shades the courtyard and the second-floor terraces (top, above).

DOUBLE HOUSE
ESPOO, FINLAND

Kristian Gullichsen and Erkki Kairamo were among the leaders of the constructivist movement that emerged in Finland in the late 1960s and '70s. This movement in turn emanated from the rationalist tendencies of the post–World War II years, which emerged as a result of the industrial reorganization that was then in the process of significantly altering Finland's forest-based economy. As a result of pressures to build economically, the rationalists and later the constructivists turned their attention to developing and using prefabricated systems. The young architects of the 1950s even exhibited an impatience with the romanticism and organic individualism of Finland's preeminent modernist, Alvar Aalto. For the most part, however, they continued to share Aalto's dedication to the social and functionalist aims of the modern movement and learned from the abundant modernist vocabulary he developed. Nor did they deny, in their work, their attachment to the country's culture and especially its landscape, whose spartan beauty remains the raw canvas upon which all Finnish designs are created.

The glazed seafront elevation (right) is divided by a central plane separating the two adjoining houses.

It is interesting to note, in the work of Gullichsen and Kairamo (who joined forces with Tim Vormala to form their own office in Helsinki in 1973), somewhat differing design approaches based on similar philosophies. Gullichsen, who grew up in Aalto's Villa Mairea and worked in Aalto's office early in his career, is known for his interest in the wall and its sculptural and light-reflecting properties. Kairamo, on the other hand, is known for his attention to line and the structural frame, and it is the latter emphasis that is apparent in the houses the firm has designed in the Helsinki suburb of Espoo since the early 1970s.

The entrance path along the side of the house (above) runs past the patio and second-floor deck, which are located in the protected area between the carport and the house (facing page).

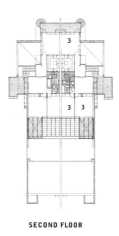

SECOND FLOOR

FIRST FLOOR
1 LIVING ROOM
2 DINING ROOM
3 BEDROOM

Most of the firm's Espoo houses are based on a core of prefabricated parts, elaborated by custom-made elements. Stairs, including spiral ones, and balconies add a residential presence to the basic rhythmic modularity of the prefabricated core. The latest of the Espoo houses, the two-family house shown on these pages, is a most dynamic example of Kairamo's work. Its envelope, more sculptural than the earlier houses, generates an impression of continuity between the interior and exterior forms and spaces.

The central wall divides the already fairly narrow coastal site lengthwise into two, and the resultant directional thrust establishes the energy of the design. The 4,800-square-foot building, then, contains two mirror-image units, each offering family privacy and views to the sea. The main living spaces, used as both living and dining rooms, run long and lean alongside the central wall from private courtyards protected by carports on the south to the sea at the north. At the north end of each house, adjacent to the living space, is a library that extends two stories from the main level to the bedroom level above. The basement level contains a swimming pool and sauna for each family.

The two-story library (facing page) is overseen from the hall above (above).

The building's harmonious order is established by the line and the plane, as embodied in the central wall slicing through and beyond the building itself, the delicate window frames, the light exterior stairs, and the screenlike handrails defining space precisely and fluidly. But it is the manner in which natural light is introduced that imparts a sense of spirituality to the design: the large north-facing windows allow the interiors to be suffused with a gentle light, even as they dissolve the boundary between house and landscape. ▪

206

Setbacks, balconies, and spiral staircases enliven the north-facing lakeside elevation, as seen both from the outside (facing page and above) and from within the double-height library (top, above).

NIALL MCLAUGHLIN ARCHITECT
LONDON

This small house, or "shack" as the architect Niall McLaughlin calls it, makes explicit reference not only to the history of the site—a former U.S. reconnaissance base from World War II—but also to its owner's occupation, photography. Depending on the viewer, the 800-square-foot retreat takes on the appearance variously of some fantastic flying machine or a telescopic camera lens. The technological ingenuity that gives rise to these visual metaphors suggests a love of innovation for its own sake, together with an almost sensual pleasure not just in what is made but how it is made. The winglike roof is constructed of an experimental combination of plywood, fiberglass, polycarbonate, and metal tethered to the ground by slender steel rods that bow the flat roof sheets into a gentle curve. The roof, anchored by a glass lantern—or is it a cockpit?—is free to flex and flap in the strong winds that sweep across the site.

From a distance, the studio appears to have landed lightly in the fields (above). Its flexible, segmented roof (facing page) moves in the wind.

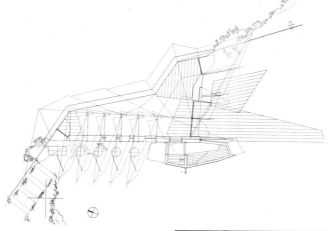

The building's simple program—photographer's studio, sauna, and sleeping space to complement the main house on the same site—allowed for another type of experimentation. The structure was built referring only to models and photographic collages (appropriately enough) without the use of conventional construction documents. The ostensibly "natural" setting of pond and field is not natural at all but man-made: the site was littered with debris that included a buried bomber plane. It is therefore impossible to determine whether the building was designed for the site, or the site for the building. Again, the photography metaphor is deliberately drawn in the still reflective water of the pond and the smooth blind wall that floats above it like a large screen. Across this surface plays an ever-changing pattern of light and shadow, raw materials for both photography and architecture. ∎

210

The lantern and skylights bring light into the interior (facing page and above). At the water's edge, a blank wall reflects patterns of sky, light, and shade (following pages).

From the street, only the garage (left) and the ramped entrance pavilion are visible on a car deck that forms the roof of the single-story house beneath it.

HOUSE IN **BRASSCHAAT** ANTWERP, BELGIUM

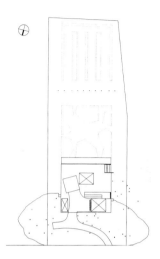

Designed for a posh suburb of Antwerp, this house by Xaveer De Geyter sums up the ambivalence many contemporary architects feel toward suburbia. Here can be found both tacit acceptance of and rebellion against the norms of suburban life. Surrounded by a "neighborhood" of opulent bourgeois "castles" designed to draw attention to themselves, this 4,800-square-foot house is radically self-effacing, literally withdrawing into the ground. Having accepted the inevitability of suburban zoning—in this wealthy enclave, a matter of huge houses on large lots—it proceeds to shut out the surrounding suburb completely, first with a sand dune separating the lot from the street, then with a red-and-white automatic automobile barrier that seals off the driveway from the road. At the same time the house itself is a trenchant commentary on suburban alienation and the main instrument of its enforcement—the automobile.

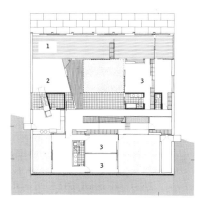

1 LIVING ROOM
2 DINING ROOM
3 BEDROOM

Playful porthole windows light the entrance ramp (above and facing page, top), which leads down to the main living spaces. These rooms open to a covered wood deck and Japanese-style courtyard (facing page, bottom).

De Geyter gives ironic, iconic significance to the car, which is both symbol and source of suburban de-urbanization: in this design, the car comes first, both literally and figuratively, and the house second. In fact, the car has a home of its own; it is protected in a translucent pavilion, like a jewel in its case, on the entry-level roof of the house. This roof plinth becomes a kind of horizontal facade, penetrated by the entrance ramp, which is housed in a triangulated pavilion whose porthole windows add an unexpected whimsy. The house is a kind of upside-down Villa Savoye, mirroring the 1929 design by Le Corbusier. At Brasschaat, as in Savoye, the car dominates the ground plane. In Le Corbusier's version, the house is lifted, and the ground is consecrated to the car, while occupants ascend by ramps or stairs to the house and ultimately a roof garden. In contrast, De Geyter lets the car occupy the roof; his visitors descend into the earth, to a garden beneath the car temple. The house's "other world" centers upon a Zen-like contemplative patio of raked gravel, opening southward to a very private landscape.

218

Some views of the house border on the surreal, especially those of the garage and entrance pavilions, which are set like toys on the flat rooftop.

There are in fact three threads of modernism that come together in this design. The rear, south-facing facade and the free-flowing organization of rooms behind it are reminiscent of the domestic designs of Mies van der Rohe, especially his Tugendhat House. The plan would appear more related to Le Corbusier than Mies van der Rohe, its square bisected by a ramp, as in the square floor plan of Villa Savoye. The house's nonhierarchical and casually functional organization, however, is derived from neither Mies van der Rohe nor Le Corbusier, but parallels the work of O.M.A. and Rem Koolhaas, with whom De Geyter has collaborated frequently, including work on the Villa dall'Ava (page 68), which was designed concurrently with Brasschaat.

The plan is best understood as a series of five zones running parallel to the road, in which living spaces alternate with service spaces. Closest to the northern, roadside edge are the children's bedrooms, interspersed with two open-air patios; then a service zone made up of the ramp and kitchen; a buffer zone that contains bathrooms, a pantry, and paved patio space; a living zone, comprised of the master bedroom, the patio and dining room, and finally the living room, office, and contemplative "tea house." The transition from zone to zone is articulated by changes in material, from carpet to vinyl to concrete, tile, or wood.

The house becomes progressively more and more open until it dissolves into the garden, designed by landscape designer Yves Brunier, who also created the garden for Villa dall'Ava. Here in this secluded garden all ties to the surrounding suburbia are cut, save for the silhouettes of the garage and the entrance pavilion, which rise above the house like sentries on guard against the outside world. ∎

JOSÉ ANTONIO MARTÍNEZ LAPEÑA AND
ELÍAS TORRES TUR, ARCHITECTS
BARCELONA

Little known abroad, architects José Antonio Martínez Lapeña and Elías Torres Tur have long exercised considerable influence as architects and teachers in Barcelona. Working for several decades on a series of projects on the resort island of Ibiza, they have built up an œuvre that is unusual in its breadth of program and in its duration. Though not the first nor the largest project designed by the architects on Ibiza, the Cap Martinet House is nonetheless seminal, representing a moment in which the architects' interest in plasticity, or the fluid manipulation of form, intersects perfectly with their study of the wall as the defining element in architecture.

The house is an essay in the definition of space by line or, in three-dimensional execution, by plane. The plan of this 2,650-square-foot house is exuberantly expressionistic. Early sketches reveal a square in plan, rotated on the steep hillside site. Traces of the square are still evident in the final version. Overlaid on this orthogonal diagram is a pinwheel of lines radiating from a center point. What appears random is not. Instead, the splayed walls have been carefully positioned either to capture and frame views of the surrounding countryside or to protect the house and its inhabitants from the view of neighbors very close by.

221

Movement through the house follows a spiral (facing page, top and bottom). The square niches in the dining room wall (facing page, middle) are echoed in punched openings in the masonry walls protecting a private courtyard (above).

It is easier to understand the house in terms of movement than of rooms. From the porte cochere, one moves into and through the house in a spiral, passing first by the kitchen, which faces the road, and then by the dining room, before arriving in the living room. Having paused here, visitors may follow the flow of space out onto a terrace, where views to the south and east reach to the horizon. More private spaces—the master bedroom, bath, and study—are folded around this spiral, with the children's and guest bedrooms and the garage one floor below. The broad, open views of the countryside from the public family spaces are replaced in these private rooms by more intimate enclosed light courts, their walls punctured by small openings that let in light but break up views of the surrounding countryside.

UPPER FLOOR
1 LIVING ROOM
2 DINING ROOM
3 BEDROOM

LOWER FLOOR

The plan has been compared to the 1951 Barceloneta apartment building by Catalan modernist Josep María Coderch, whose influence Lapeña and Torres readily acknowledge. It is also easy to see in this house the shadow of Barcelona's eccentric premodernist Antonio Gaudí, whose Parc Güell has been restored over a ten-year period under the direction of Lapeña and Torres. Critics have written of the serendipitous mix of the more rational, controlled Lapeña with the extroverted, freewheeling Torres. The Cap Martinet House is a perfect blend of both tendencies; its rational, orthogonal side is evident, for example, in the gridded cabinet wall in the dining room, while the walls extending into the landscape imply openness and exuberance.

These white walls are also the perfect foil for the Mediterranean sun. The house sacrifices none of its modernity in this attentive response to context. The use of local stone at the entrance and in the retaining walls, and the color scheme—white, yellow, and a very Mediterranean blue—bow to local tradition. (The yellow and white entranceway also nods to a house by Josep Lluis Sert directly across the street.) Born and raised in Ibiza, Torres has a special relationship with the island, and in projects ranging from the restoration of the church of l'Hospitalet and the Ibiza castle to apartments and several houses, Lapeña and Torres have done more, perhaps, than any other contemporary architects to define the nature of this place. ∎

The expressionist plans shape a pinwheel of walls extending beyond the house and its terraces into the landscape.

226

The careful framing of specific views from the terraces is accomplished by white walls, which shape dynamic exterior spaces. These white planes form striking compositions against the blue Mediterranean sky.

HOUSE AND STUDIO ROTTERDAM, THE NETHERLANDS

Architect Francine Houben of the Dutch firm Mecanoo does not like to be labeled a modernist. "We take an independent position; we do not work dogmatically," she says. Resisting what they consider to be the rhetoric of late-twentieth-century modernism and its excessive dedication to formalism, Mecanoo instead emphasizes the problem-solving side of architecture and its social dimension, both of which were important topics for early modernism. The firm got its first commission while the principals were still in architecture school, when they won a competition in 1983 to design a housing development in Rotterdam. Although Mecanoo has since designed many other building types, including a highly praised library in Almelo, they remain best known for multiunit housing and urban design. This 3,000-square-foot house outside Rotterdam, designed by Houben with then-partner Erick van Egeraat as their own home and studio, is the firm's only single-family commission.

The grid of solid and void, of lines and flat planes, that makes up the street facade is most crisply visible at night.

GROUND FLOOR

1/2

FIRST FLOOR

1 LIVING ROOM

2 DINING ROOM

3 BEDROOM

SECOND FLOOR

A bamboo screen shades the glass side wall (above). The living, dining, and kitchen areas occupy the main floor (facing page, top) with a library on the top floor (facing page, bottom).

The house is undeniably sensible in its organization and industrial in its construction. Nevertheless, simple functionalism alone cannot fully explain the equally undeniable aesthetic dimension of a design that goes beyond programmatic necessity to achieve unusual compositional balance and delicacy. The house occupies a unique site bounded in two directions by water. To the north, the street facade faces a small lake. To the south, the rear elevation overlooks a canal that runs perpendicular to the house and parallel to a row of typical Dutch rowhouses. These conventional nineteenth-century structures, with their pitched tile roofs and brick facades, are the perfect foils for Mecanoo's late-twentieth-century composition of glass, steel, and wood. A narrow, empty strip that separates the house from its next-door neighbor and provides rear access seems to mark the line between centuries as well.

The ground floor is occupied by a garage, studio, and entrance hall. The top two floors are conceived as a unit connected by a double-height space at the heart of the house that provides both light and circulation. The main living and dining spaces are raised to the second floor to take advantage of the lake views; above them, a large library is connected by a catwalk across the double-height opening to one of three bedrooms on the top floor.

Van Egeraat, who has since left Mecanoo, and Houben traveled to Japan shortly before designing this house, and the influence of Japanese architecture, long a source of inspiration to modern architects, is very apparent. The rear garden, with its circular splash pond, is overtly Japanese in flavor and detail. The bamboo cane screen that moves on an aluminum track to shield glazing on the east wall is a clever and beautiful interpretation of Japanese shoji screens.

The ground-floor studio opens to a Japanese-style garden (facing page and above).

Each floor is organized to maximize transparency through the house from water to water. Service elements such as bathrooms, kitchen, and entry stair are concentrated at the western edge of the site, along a blank wall that narrowly separates the house from its neighbor. The connection between the upper two floors is strongly evident on the street facade, which appears to be a single sheet of glass, fronted by a pair of thin metal balconies beneath the roof's sheltering overhang. The south or rear facade is more horizontal in nature, its composition a grid of glass and wood infill panels with balconies that extend interior space both visually and physically. The play of opaque and transparent materials and the shifting patterns of light and shade enhanced by awnings and overhangs transform all three principal facades into intricate gridded compositions that, wittingly or not, recall De Stijl, the Dutch contribution to modernism. ∎

234

The rear facade overlooks neighboring nineteenth-century townhouses and a typical Dutch canal.